SECRETS OF AST
BASED ON HINDU A

Secrets of Astrology is a ready reckoner for the lay reader to find solutions to his problems. It tells him how to know his own personality and that of his spouse, friends, and others. It gives tips on how to choose one's ideal life-partner. Love marriages, delayed marriages and divorce are also dealt with, as are lucky numbers and colours according to one's personality.

Love, character and sex have been discussed with the help of a Lover's Guide and sex-life barometers, linking the signs and showing how opposite signs attract each other.

Guidance is provided about predicting lucky times to acquire money, property and conveyance, win lotteries and make gains from horse-racing. Travel, employment, business, children, politics and spiritual ty are other subjects on which clear directions are given.

To overcome difficulties, remedial measures, including use of tested Yantra, Mantra and Tantra, are prescribed.

Dr. L.R. Chawdhri has an experience of 39 years in the fields of Astrology, Palmistry and Numerology. He has specialised in remedial measures developed by these sciences. He is author of 17 widely acclaimed books on occult subjects.

By the same author:

Secrets of Occult Science: How to read Omens, Moles, Dreams and Handwriting

Secrets of Yantra, Mantra and Tantra

SECRETS OF ASTROLOGY
BASED ON HINDU ASTROLOGY

DR. L.R. Chawdhri

A Sterling Paperback

STERLING PAPERBACKS
An imprint of
Sterling Publishers (P) Ltd.
A-59, Okhla Industrial Area, Phase-II,
New Delhi-110020.
Tel: 26387070, 26386209; Fax: 91-11-26383788
E-mail: mail@sterlingpublishers.com
www.sterlingpublishers.com

Secrets of Astrology—Based on Hindu Astrology
© 1989, Dr. L.R. Chawdhri
ISBN 978 81 207 6880 2
Reprint 2005, 2006, 2007, 2012

Printed in India

Printed and Published by Sterling Publishers Pvt. Ltd.,
New Delhi-110 020.

PREFACE

This book, based on Hindu astrology, aims to cater to the general interest of the public and serve as a guide to students of this science in predicting accurately incidents and events shaping the lives of men and women. It deals with the most important aspects of human life — marriage, children, profession, finance, love, personality, etc.

The final chapter on Mantra, Yantra and Tantra brings out their beneficial effects on people using them.

Tables showing the Zodiac signs and various aspects of life are designed to help readers to know the nomenclature of planets and understand the signs terminology along with *nakshatras*, colours, gems, etc. The Ascendant Table at the end of the book provides a useful guide for readers to determine the propitious time and place for the commencement of a business venture, professional career or a journey.

In case of any difficulty, readers may contact me at my residence.

Jyotish Tantra Kendra   **Dr. L.R. Chawdhri**
110, Pratap Chambers,
Gurudwara Road,
Karol Bagh,
New Delhi - 110005

CONTENTS

1

ASTROLOGY AND ITS USES

The word "Astrology" is derived from two Greek words, "Astra" and "Logos", logic or reason. It literally implies the doctrine and law as shown by the Stars or Planets. It is a science of influence of stars on human and terrestrial affairs. It is a science which defines the actions of celestial bodies upon animate and inanimate objects, and their reactions to such influences. Astrology may be considered as subjective, dealing with the influence on various forms of life and its effects upon surrounding bodies, the Earth and its inhabitants in particular, and so may properly be termed, the study of Life's Reactions to Planetary Vibrations.

Astrology is a noble science as old as the ages of Vedas. This was founded, investigated and developed by our ancient Maharishis. The pioneers mentioned are Aryabhatta, Maharishi Parashar, Varahamihira, Garga, Kalidasa, Kalyan Verma and other sages etc. who lived about 1500 B.C. and made a special study of Astrology in relation to various aspects of human life including health, diseases, deaths etc.

It depends on the positions of planets ascertained. Astronomically, it is derived from the observation and study of the celestial bodies of which our earth is one. It is a "Message of Stars". It is a Divine Science of Correspondences in that it applies Cosmic Principles to the minutiae of everyday life, system of interpretation of planetary action in human experiences. Our sages noted a close correspondence between the great world of universe and the microcosm or the little world of man well expressed in the hermetic axiom. Astrology has lived through the ages in countries like, India, Egypt, Arabia, USA, China, Chalden, Rome, Babylon, Greece, etc. If it is not true or scientific how has it stood for such a long time against many and heavy odds?

Is Astrology Scientific?

In addition to the above discussion, we know from ancient times, that planets affect human beings and that was not accepted by many scientists, but later after experiments, observations and experience they found that Electronic Radiations from the heavenly bodies produce molecular change in earth's atmosphere and produce cellular change in organic bodies of all dwellings therein, so says Rodney Collin. Now scientists agree a bit (why not fully?) of all knowledge bequeathed to us by our sages and ancients. Dr. Charles Nordmon has expressed, "X-rays coming from stars which abundantly emit those rays exercise influence on the life organisms of each of us."

Ralph Waldo Emerson wrote, "Astronomy brought to earth and applied to the affairs of men. Of what use is Astronomy to mankind, if not interpreted in terms of our daily life?"

Great writers of the world Dante, Shakespeare, Longfellow, Goethe, Milton, Tennyson, Keats, Dryden and Chaucer used astrological dictums in their works. The distinguished Danish astronomer Tycho used his astronomical knowledge in his astrological studies. There are many more such personalities.

Scientists of today follow Newton, his laws and his findings, but do not follow his astrological findings. Why? It is quite ridiculous and this attitude is not understood. The scientists who have not studied the subject have no right to be biased against it.

Our ancient sages had studied astrology and have framed the rules to predict about personal matters, diseases, weather forecastings, calamities, coronations, wars, rains, earthquakes, personal and other orbit incidents which are correct even today and cannot be denied.

The critics and scientists are against astrology as if this science is their rival. It can be due to their ignorance of the subject. But do they know that many times their experiments have failed, many satellites have failed to take off causing loss of crores of rupees to the nation? In such cases are we to blame science?

Astrology is regarded highly throughout the world. Great Swiss psychologist Dr. Carl G. Jung has testified to this science being worthy. Hippocrates, hailed as the father of medicine, went so far as to assert that a doctor without astrological knowledge cannot safely administer medicine. But look at the modern doctors!

Another eye-catching example is of the politicians. They consult the astrologers and are benefited, but on a public platform they hesitate and feel shy to acknowledge it. Revelation of Mrs. Reagan's obsession with astrology and President Reagan's acceptance of it shocked and fascinated the people all over the world. But Reagan is not the first head of the State to believe in astrology. President Mitterand of France has admitted that he is an avid reader of Nostradamus, the French seer, astrologer who lived 400 years ago. Mrs. Indira Gandhi is known to have consulted astrologers before taking any major decision. Recently, the popularity of Orsen Wells' programme on Nostradamus on American TV has surprised many. According to a former CIA official, the American Intelligence Agency has also used astrology in its operations (*Evening News*, August 2, 1988)

The idea of the above discussion indicates that probabilities are in every science. The press and the people have a tendency to exaggerate wrong prediction and hold it against astrology whereas failures of scientists causing loss of crores of rupees to the nation goes unnoticed. So the Government should not be persistent in calling astrology as a science. This science should be given due place in the Universities, in science labs which should be provided in sufficient numbers as there is wider scope for astrological research and everyone wants to have something new.

We now gather that astrology is a recognised science since times immemorial.

Use of Astrology

Astrology is as important to male or female as is psychology. This branch of knowledge deals with the human soul deriving awareness of the mind from the careful examination of the facts of consciousness. Astrology complements everything in psychology because it examines the facts of planetary influences on the conscious and subconscious, providing a guideline towards all aspects of life, harmony of mind, body and spirit. This is the real use of astrology.

SUN SIGN—Sun sign in astrology has become the roaring chariot, with spokes of golden fire; the influence of Sun has woven into the

horoscopes of a new generation of people who has only a vague idea
about astrology.

As interest in astrology escalated with the modern generation, so
the Sun sign theme rose in popularity and became a piece of
conversation at parties. Now a Virgo man complains that he is very
different from another Virgo man and proves that astrology is nothing
but a hoax. Actually this is not so, only the Sun sign will not help you.
You have to check Ascendant, Moon sign, placement of other planets in
the horoscope, which affect the Sun sign that changes the personality
very radically.

Due to a constant flow of the astrological journals, columns in
newspapers, the people have become Sun-sign-conscious. Such
readings are too general and are not applicable to everybody but on the
other hand misguides people and astrology is defamed. As an example
when one discovers that he/she is a Leo, they imagine him/her as a
passionate lover, but this is not always correct.

So do not depend on Sun sign only. You must get your horoscope
checked by a competent astrologer. Sun or Solar horoscope cast from
date of birth is not the real birth chart but a fiction because the real
Ascendant, mid-heaven etc. cannot be cast correctly.

MOON SIGN—Our ancients have advocated the use of Moon sign
(Janam Rasi) which gives fairly more accurate results than the Sun sign.
This sign is very important in Hindu astrology for matching the
horoscopes to see whether one might be happier with a boy or a girl, as
the Moon indicates many of one's basic reactions to both sexes.

There are other branches of astrology like Medical astrology,
Mundane or Political astrology etc.

So, astrology being a perfect science, can be usefully employed in
the delineation of one's horoscope through a competent astrologer.

BASIC RULES OF ASTROLOGY

The zodiac is a circle of space surrounding the earth and is an imagined belt in the heavens in which the planets travel or as is commonly understood as the apparent path of the Sun round the earth, i.e. elliptic. It is invisible.

The zodiac has been divided into twelve parts of 30 degrees each, each part is called a Sign comprising 30 degrees of celestial longitude. The planets travel in its orbit, going from one sign to another and completing the whole zodiac.

We provide a Table of Zodical signs and their elements indicating month etc. as per Hindu Astrology.

THE ASTERISM OR NAKSHATRA

A Nakshatra or an Asterism is a group of stars found in the sky. According to the ancient astrological canons, the zodiac is divided into 27 sections, the area of which has been marked by a particular star, located close to the zodiac belt; such a section is called Asterism or in Sanskrit, Nakshatra.

These are of great importance in Hindu astrology where many things are worked out by the Nakshatras. The Western astrologers always calculate in terms of signs and cusps and when they speak of the zodiac, they always mean the elliptic Sun's path.

These Nakshatras are grouped into triads and a planet is said to rule each triad. The name of each Nakshatra, his extent, the planets that rule the same and their respective periods are tabulated on page 7 and these should be memorised for further use, particularly the number of each Nakshatra.

Zodiac Signs and Their Elements

SIGN	Aries	Taurus	Gemini	Cancer	Leo	Virgo	Libra	Scorpio	Sagittarius	Capricorn	Aquarius	Pisces
Symbols	♈	♉	♊	♋	♌	♍	♎	♏	♐	♑	♒	♓
No	1	2	3	4	5	6	7	8	9	10	11	12
Ruler	Mars	Venus	Mercury	Moon	Sun	Mercury	Venus	Mars	Jupiter	Saturn	Saturn	Jupiter
Detriment	Venus	Mars	Jupiter	Saturn	-	-	Mars	Venus	Mecurry	Moon	Sun	Mercury
Exaltation	Sun	Moon	Rahu	Jupiter	-	Mercury	Saturn	Moon	Ketu	Mars	-	Venus
Fall	Saturn	-	Katu	Mars	-	Venus	Sun	-	Rahu	Jupiter	-	Mercury
Constitution	Movable	Fixed	Common	Movable	Fixed	Common	Movable	Fixed	Common	Movable ?	Movable	Common
Element	Fiery	Earthy	Airy	Watery	Fiery	Earthy	Airy	Watery	Fiery	Earthy	Airy	Watery
Human-body	Head	Neck	Arms	Breast	Spine	Abdominal	Lumber	Secrets	Hips	Knees	Legs	Feet
Month (Hindi)	Vaisakh	Jeshth	Asar	Savan	Bhadron	Aswij	Kartik	Maghsar	Pause	Magh	Phagun	Chaitra
Type	Malefic	Benefic	Malefic	Benefic	Malefic	Benefic	Malefic	Benefic	Malefic	Benefic	Malefic	Benefic
Ascension	Long	Short	Average	Long	Long	Long	Long	Long	Long	Average	Short	Short
Direction	East	South	West	North	East	South	West	North	East	South	West	North
Constellations	Aswini Bhami Kritika 1	Kritika 3. Rohini Mriga 2	Mriga 2 Aridra Punur 3	Punur 1 Pushy Ashelsha	Makha P.Phalg U. Phalg 1	U. Pholg 3 Hast Chitra 1	Chitra 2 Swati Vaisakha3	Vaisakha1 Anuradha Jeshita	Vaisakha1 Moola P.Shada U. Shada (1) .. ta 2	U. Shada 3 Dhanishta Sarvana U. Sha- Dhanish ta 2	Dhanishta 2 Satbhisha P. Bha dra 3	P. Bhadra 1 U.Bladra Rewati
Colour	Red	white	green	white	orange	yellow	Rose	Brown	yellow	Black	Indigo	Violet

Note:
Kendra Houses 1, 4, 7,10
Kona Houses 5, 9,
Oopachaya Houses 3, 6, 10, 11

Sirshodya signs 3, 5, 6, 7, 7, 11
Prishodya signs 1, 2, 4, 9, 10

Cadent sign 2, 5, 7, 11
Succedent 1, 3, 6, 9, 12

TABLE OF NAKSHATRAS

No.	Name of Nakshatra	Western Name	Extent in signs From	To	Period of Nakshatra	Ruler of Nakshatra
			S 0 /	S 0 /	Y M	
1.	Aswini	Arietic	0 0 0	0 13 20	2—4	Ketu
2.	Bharni	Triangalara	0 13 20	0 26 40	6—8	Venus
3.	Krittika	Pleiades	0 26 40	1 10 0	2—0	Sun
4.	Rohini	Aldebran	1 10 0	1 23 20	3—4	Moon
5.	Mrigasira	Orionis	1 23 20	2 6 40	2—4	Mars
6.	Aridra	Betelgeuse	2 6 40	2 20 0	6—0	Rahu
7.	Punarvasu	Pollux	2 20 0	3 3 20	5—4	Jupiter
8.	Pushyami	Castor	3 3 20	3 6 40	6—4	Saturn
9.	Aslesha	Hydrae	3 6 40	4 0 0	5—8	Mercury
10.	Magha	Regulas	4 0 0	4 13 20	2—4	Ketu
11.	Poorva Phalguni	Zosma	4 13 20	4 26 40	6—8	Venus
12.	Uttra Phalguni	Denebala	4 26 40	5 10 0	2—0	Sun
13.	Hast	Corvas	5 10 0	5 23 20	3—4	Moon
14.	Chitra	Spica	5 23 20	6 6 40	6—0	Mars
15.	Swati	Arcturus	6 6 40	6 20 0	5—4	Rahu
16.	Vaisakha	Zubemubi	6 20 0	7 3 20	6—4	Jupiter
17.	Anuradha	Scorpius	7 3 20	7 16 40	5—8	Saturn
18.	Jyeshtha	Antares	7 16 40	8 0 0	2—4	Mercury
19.	Moola	Shaula	8 0 0	8 13 20	6—8	Ketu
20.	Poorva Shada	Kaus-Aust	8 13 20	8 26 40	2—0	Venus
21.	Uttra Shada	Nunki	8 26 40	9 10 0	3—4	Sun
22.	Sarvana	Altair	9 10 0	9 23 20	2—4	Moon
23.	Dhamishta	Delphinus	9 23 20	10 6 40	2—4	Mars
24.	Satbhisha	Aquari	10 6 40	10 20 0	6—0	Rahu
25.	Poorva Bhadra	Pegasus	10 20 0	11 3 20	5—4	Jupiter
26.	Uttra Bhadra	Pegas	11 3 20	11 16 40	6—4	Saturn
27.	Rewati	Piscium	11 16 40	0 0 0	5—8	Mercury

USE OF TITHIS

The Tithi is the distance between Moon and Sun. It is the phase of Moon and is called Lunar day. Moon completes the zodiac in 27 days time as Moon remains in one sign for 2• days. The changes or phases are the results of the changing positions of Moon and Earth in relation to Sun. Sometimes Moon is between Sun and Earth and other times Earth is between Sun and Moon.

These phases indicate Full Dark Moon to Full Moon or in Hindu Astrology called Amavasya to Poornima respectively and the periods are called Krishna Paksha and Shukla Paksha respectively. In each period there are 14 tithis besides Amavasya and Poornima.

To find out the tithi, deduct the longitude of Sun from Moon. If difference is more than 180 degrees, it is Dark half or Krishna Paksha and if the difference is less than 180 degrees, it is Bright half or Shukla Paksha. Divide the difference by 12 degrees. The quotient represents the number of tithis elapsed and the remainder the part of the next (current) tithi.

In Hindu Astrology tithi is used in day-to-day life specially in Muhurtas (Auspicious time to do a work).

1. The 4th, 8th, 12th and 14th lunar days or tithis both in Dark and Bright half are unsuitable for doing or starting any auspicious work.

2. The 4th, 6th, 8th or 12th tithis of Full Moon days should be avoided for starting any work or journey, etc.

3. Religious propitiations are necessary if the birth is during the last 48 minutes or four-fifths of an hour of Panchmi or lunar day, Dashami or 10th lunar day, Amavas or 30th lunar day, Poornima or Full Moon day or 15th lunar day, for the longevity and prosperity of the native.

4. Krishna Chaturdashi or 14th day of Dark half is of importance. First one-sixth period is auspicious.

5. Successful or Sidha tithis have been deemed as beneficial. Business or any auspicious work undertaken in these tithis result in success. If tithi coincides with a day, as shown below, the tithi is termed as "Sidha", in either Paksha.

Tithi	Week Days
3,8,13	Tuesday
2,7,12	Wednesday
5,10,15	Thursday
1,6,11	Friday
4,9,14	Saturday

The following are names of tithis in Hindu Astrology in either Paksha.

Tithi	Hindu Name	Tithi	Hindu Name
1	Partipat	8	Ashtami
2	Davitya	9	Naumi
3	Tritiya	10	Dasami
4	Chaturthi	11	Ekadashi
5	Panchmi	12	Dwadasi
6	Sasthi	13	Trayodasi
7	Saptami	14	Chaturdasi
		15	Amavas or Poornima

SUN'S PASSAGE IN WESTERN AND HINDU ASTROLOGY

Sun's position in a horoscope is most important but baffles many serious lovers of astrology. In newspapers, journals, magazines and other literature, forecasting weekly events are based on Sun Sign, viz. the position of Sun in your horoscope at birth time. There are two types of dates based on Western Astrology as per *Sayana System* and on Hindu Astrology based on *Niryana System*. The reader who checks the position of Sun sign in his birth chart will find Sun sign different in both cases. In Hindu Astrology, the Sun sign is based on Niryana System, which will be followed in this book. Usually, there is a difference of one sign in either system.

No	Sign	Indian Month	Indian Dates Niryana System	Western Dates Sayana System	Position of Sun in Nakshatra
1.	Aries	Vaisakha	13th April - 14th May	March, 21—April 21	Vaisakha
2.	Taurus	Jesth	15th May - 14th June	April 22—May 20	Jyestha
3.	Gemini	Asar	15th June - 14th July	May 21—June 21	Purva Asadha
4.	Cancer	Sarvana	15th July - 14th August	June 22—July 22	Sarvana
5.	Leo	Bhadra	15th August - 15th Sept.	July 23—August 23	Purva Bhadra
6.	Virgo	Aswij	16th Sept. - 15th Oct.	August 24—Sept. 23	Aswini
7.	Libra	Kartik	16th Oct. - 14th Nov.	Sept. 24—Oct. 23	Kartika
8.	Scorpio	Maghsar	15th Nov. - 14th Dec.	Oct. 24—Nov. 22	Mrigasira or Aridra
9.	Sagittarius	Pause	15th Dec. - 13th Jan.	Nov. 23—Dec. 21	Pushyami
10.	Capricorn	Magh	14th Jan. - 12th Feb.	Dec. 22—Jan. 21	Magha
11.	Aquarius	Phagun	13th Feb. - 12th March	Jan. 22—Feb. 19	Uttra Phalguni
12.	Pisces	Chitra	13th March - 12th April	Feb 19—March 20	Chitra

The table provided on page 9 will clarify the position. According to Hindu system, Sun enters Aries on 13th April, on Vaisakha a Hindu month and this day is called "Baisakhi".

From the table, you will also find that names of Indian months are in consonance with the Nakshatras in which Moon travels during the sign period. All things are interconnected in Hindu system of Astrology.

Due to elliptical orbit Poornima (Full Moon Day) does not take place in same position or in the same Nakshatra every year. For instance, Moon in Poornima in the month of Maghsar may be in Aridra or Mrigasira Nakshatra. So the month of Agrahayana has another name Maghsar.

MOON THROUGH SIGNS

In Hindu astrology Moon has special significance which is in transit to different signs. In these signs, the position of Moon somewhere is very auspicious for certain important works or inauspicious indicating troubles, illness and loss etc. These are indicated below:

	Sign	Auspicious Degrees	Inauspicious Degrees
1.	Aries	21st degree	8th or 26th degrees
2.	Taurus	14th "	25th or 12th "
3.	Gemini	18th "	22nd or 13th "
4.	Cancer	8th "	22nd or 25th "
5.	Leo	19th "	21st or 24th "
6.	Virgo	9th "	1st or 11th "
7.	Libra	24th "	4th or 26th "
8.	Scorpio	11th "	23rd or 14th "
9.	Sagittarius	23rd "	18th or 13th "
10.	Capricorn	14th "	20th or 25th "
11.	Aquarius	19th "	20th or 5th "
12.	Pisces	9th "	10th or 12th "

So we have seen so far that zodiacal signs, Nakshatra, Sun and Moon have definite place in astrology. Birth of the native in a particular sign, Nakshatra, Sun sign and Moon sign have a great bearing on one's life. The details of these you will find in the subsequent chapters.

HOUSES AND PLANETS

The zodiac is divided into 12 signs and each sign has one house. So the whole life has been divided and contained in 12 houses which is explained as follows:

Signification of Houses

1st House: This house is called Ascendant or Lagna, its lord is called Lagnesh. This house signifies life, longevity, self, health, nature and appearance of native. Complexion, vitality, sorrows, gains and profits to younger brothers and his friends. It governs head and face.

2nd House: This house indicates inflow of finances, bank position, right eye, family, early age or boyhood, speech, sanyas, servants and friends. Self earned wealth, loss or damage, worldly possessions, jewellery, grandfather and mother. It also denotes family, eyesight, understanding with family members, inheritance, law suits, throat, right eye, domestic comforts in general.

3rd House: It denotes younger brothers and sisters and their relations. It signifies courage, intelligence, education up to Higher Secondary level, taste for writing, ornaments, clothes, short journeys. Signing contracts and documents etc. Body parts are arms, right ear, shoulders etc.

4th House: This house signifies mother, property, conveyance, domestic surroundings and happiness. Old age environments, private affairs, public, inheritance, false allegations, agriculture land and its produce. It represents breasts, chest, lung, stomach, elbow joints etc.

5th House: Children, speculation, intellectual status and luck are gauged from this house. Pleasure, love affairs, lady love, legal or illegal amusements, kidnap, rape etc. are also checked. Belly, heart, liver, spleen are the body parts covered by this house.

6th House: This house is responsible for enemies, health, service, servants, uncle, aunts and relations on father's side. Food, subordinates, debts, obstacles in life, mental worries, theft and calamity etc. The body parts denoted are kidney, large intestine, uterus and anus

7th House: Matters regarding wife, husband, partnership, external sex organs, conjugal happiness are checked from 7th house. This house also denotes marriage, married life, love, contracts, litigations, divorce, honour and reputation in foreign country. Body parts are private parts, uterus, glands etc.

8th House: Diseases, death, finances through unfair means, internal sex organs, longevity, mental pain, obstacles, dowry of wife, gain from in-laws, mode of death, imprisonment, worries and privations are checked from 8th house. It indicates body parts as scrotum, pelvis, seminal vesicles, external genetalia, etc.

9th House: This house indicates religion, foreign travel, publicity, preceptor, higher education, learnings, writing books, also faith, wisdom, prosperity, powers of foresight, religious institutions, providential help, etc. Hips, thighs are body parts.

10th House: This important house indicates father, profession, status in life, activities outside house, pleasures, honour, power and authority, Government favour, trade, business, command, honour, occupation, adopted son. All questions regarding worldly activities and moral responsibilities. Body parts are knees, joints, bones, hairs and back.

11th House: It accounts for accumulated wealth, elder brothers and sisters and relations with them. Friends, fluctuating money gains, club or social activities, emotional attachments, love affairs and friends, honour, social success etc. Body parts are legs, left ear, teeth, ankle etc.

12th House: It signifies private enemies, pleasures of beds, law suits, imprisonments, secret works, moksha, hospitalisation, conjugal relations with opposite sex other than legitimate. Sorrows, debts, lost goods etc. are judged. Body parts are feet, left eye, teeth etc.

SIGNIFICATION OF PLANETS IN HOUSES

The Planets in Hindu Astrology is called "Graha" and all the nine planets are known as "Nava Graha" which include Sun, Moon (Luminaries), Mercury, Venus, Mars, Jupiter and Saturn, Rahu and Ketu which are shadowy planets as they possess no material bodies.

Each Graha or Planet represents its own characteristics. It represents ideas in active, passive, figurative or literal senses. Precisely, the entire world of ideas are represented by Nava Graha and these are explained as follows.

1. Sun

Sun signifies father, courage, power and authority, finances, ambitions, boldness, politician, commanding power, dignity, generosity and kind heartedness. Also optimism, administrator, general success, royalty, real love and personality of the native. When afflicted reverse results.

Sun in Ascendant is most auspicious. If the person is born with it in 1st house he will be bold, generous and healthy. Bold to face odds in life, of practical nature. Commanding voice and will gain through inheritance.

Sun in 2nd house will make the person rich, earning through self efforts, voracious eater, gain through Government, and persons in authority. Will hold a good position. Generous, social, fond of opposite sex and courageous.

In 3rd house great strength, fame, wealthy, success in travels, helpful to relations. Bold and bounded by family ties. Good manners and rise in life. Of constructive actions and thoughts. Popular in life.

In 4th house, one will have land, buildings, gain through inheritance, chance of honour in later period of life. Intelligent and brave.

In 5th house, honourable and successful attachments, social and of pleasure-loving nature. Good education; progeny will be less. Gain through judicious speculations.

In 6th house it denotes impaired health. Gain in service. Will have opponents and enemies.

In 7th house Sun indicates late marriage, disharmony in married life, changes in life. Relations with opposite sex.

In 8th house health will not remain good. Gain of money through illegal ways. Death can be violent. Early death of father.

In 9th house, gives prestige and position. Favours the company of right and religious persons. Luck in foreign countries.

In 10th house, it is very good for power and authority. Industrious and royal life. Ambitious and blessed with all comforts of life.

In 11th house, indicates easy money, contact with eminent persons, will be wealthy and rich. Kingly status. Popular among friends.

In 12th house, occult and psychic tendencies. Success over enemies, may like seclusion, should safeguard against fraud, enmity. Unexpected events in life will happen. False friends and accusations etc.

2. Moon

The Moon signifies mother and denotes softness, charming eyes, steady mind, generosity, menses, infants, love, pleasures, breasts, family life, beauty, watery places and passions.

Moon sign is generally used to forecast the future which is more reliable than Sun sign.

In a birth chart, when posited in 1st house makes one sensitive, restless, imaginative, inclined to public life. Likes change in residence, profession and employment, etc. Of intuitive and perceptive mind.

In 2nd house, changeable finances, success in business with general public, helpful friends, wealthy, loved by opposite sex, gain through mother.

In 3rd house, one is learned, confident, intuitive, fond of new surroundings, travels, social and knowledgable. One has good friends and pleasurable company.

In 4th house, attachment with parents, changeable circumstances and residence. Gain from parents, opposite sex and domestic life.

In 5th house, good sons, intelligent, enjoys life like a minister. Public success. Fond of children and opposite sex.

In 6th house, one has afflicted health, gain by serving others and in service. Gain through servants. Success with small animals.

In 7th house, one has good look, loved by women but of changeable affection. Of liberal views.

In 8th house, when well aspected gain through wife; is rich, intelligent, life full of enjoyment. Gain in public life and finances also.

In 9th house, the person becomes prosperous, virtuous and victorious. Fond of travels, publication, wealth and lives abroad.

In 10th house, changeable profession, is rich, has great connections. Inclined to public life. Rise and downfall in life.

In 11th house, long life, wealthy, high minded, respected, learned and blessed with power and authority, unreliable friends.

In 12th house, love of occultism, mysteries and romance. Secret missions, discreet love affairs, sensitive and likes solitude.

Conjunctions

Moon being the most important planet, we wish to provide the results of conjunction of Moon with other planets.

The Sun-Moon conjunction indicates weakness of body as well as mind. At times brings depression. If in Aries or Cancer indicates self-reliance, personal independence. Good for social acts, favours love, friendship and marriage.

Moon-Mercury—one speaks softly and sweetly, good under-standing, kind, tactful, famous, liked by ladies.

Moon-Venus—one is respected, fond of dress and amusements and opposite sex. One becomes steady and calm. Of cheerful outlook, optimistic, love of luxury.

Moon-Mars conjunction increases energy, is daring, fond of opposite sex, passionate. Gain through business. One can be a liar and of wicked deeds. It is considered Laxmiyoga (Wealth) without mental happiness. Rebellious trends can be there.

Moon-Jupiter is highly harmonious, fortunate and successful, wins over enemies, eyesight will become weak as age advances. Peace of mind and all comforts.

Moon-Saturn conjunction makes one gloomy, but best for persons who have to live as selfless workers with noble objects and are patriotic. They are careful, duty bound, favourable for organising new business. Spend money on amusements and on opposite sex.

Moon-Rahu, a malefic for the traits of house, where posited.

Moon-Ketu unfavourable results as above.

3. Mercury

Mercury is the planet of intellect, speech, memory, education, short travels, virility, wisdom, intuitive power, occult sciences etc.

In 1st house, one is humorous, quick-witted, has strong memory, sweet speech and is clever. Rich, kind hearted, fond of literature, impressive and undertakes journeys, etc.

In 2nd house gain through administration, is intelligent, wealthy, sincere, gains by writings; clerks; when afflicted, one stammers.

In 3rd house, many short journeys, gains from writing books and famous good orator, bold, of investigating nature, happy relations with all.

In 4th house, gain from inheritance and business. Changes in residence. Disturbed home affairs and worries. Property, popularity in public and success.

In 5th house, much interested in education of children. Intelligent but with much mental pressure. Gain through speculation and investments.

In 6th house, harsh in speech, disputes and loss through servants, of quarrelsome nature, journeys, logical clear mind and good in accounts, etc.

In 7th house, intelligent, cheerful marriage, gain through partnership, active, clever and progressive. If afflicted, unsettled married life.

In 8th house, intelligent, rich and famous. Supporter of family. Long life, renowned. If afflicted, denotes brain or nervous disorder and family life.

In 9th house, learned, intelligent, wealthy, good conduct, educated, success in journeys, legal affairs and publishing. Active and good speech.

In 10th house, wealthy, liberal, famous. Successful in any task one undertakes. Practical views. Good position for services and taste for literature.

In 11th house, very rich, long life, many servants and

acquaintances, but few real friends, of good organising capacity. Gain through friends.

In 12th house, work done with concentration, will be successful. Fond of research. Secret acts, occult and unusual thoughts. Enemies, love of risk and mystery. Untimely success. When afflicted, worries; scandals, devoid of learnings, of doubtful nature etc.

4. Mars

Mars has sudden, explosive and disruptive actions. It is significator of brother, energy, courage, ambitions, desires and self-confidence. Practical nature, accidents, cuts, wounds and operations.

In 1st house, one is brave, strong, respected, harsh tempered, tireless worker, ambitious, of independent views and loves liberty. Aggressive, headstrong, forceful and impatient.

In 2nd house, one is overgenerous, extravagant, earning through hard work. Harsh in speech, of amiable nature, self earned wealth, money by legacy or marriage.

In 3rd house, danger of accidents during journey. Sense of independence and egoism. Gain of wealth, is learned and brave.

In 4th house, good Mars denotes energy, force and property acquisition. One will not gain at birthplace. Domestic quarrels and unhappiness coupled with misunderstandings. Loss through fire, accident in home.

In 5th house, avoid impulsiveness, change in love, use of sexual force, rash, attraction to opposite sex, abortion, accident to 1st child and loss by speculation.

In 6th house, famous, wealthy and victorious. Afflicted health, disputes and quarrels. Losses through theft and servants. Avoid inprudence and take care of health.

In 7th house, unless well aspected, indicates improper actions, diseases, domestic peace will remain disturbed. Most passionate, impetuous in love. Death or separation of partner. In Cancer or Pisces sign, husband will be worthless with bad habits, excessively demonstrative in affection and of forceful nature causing troubles to partner.

In 8th house, if benefic and receives good aspects, then increase in property through partner, legacies or inheritance. Otherwise death due to sickness or accident. Strained relations with wife/husband may cause separation. If afflicted, losses, sudden or violent death.

In 9th house, freedom of thoughts, intellectual and philosophical insight, quite active, success in law suits, enterprising and progressive, etc.

In 10th house, gain and promotion, brave, industrious, gain from father and by legacy. Great opportunities for progress. Love of work, famous and of liberal views.

In 11th house, indicates courage, rich and happy. Fulfilment of desires and wishes. Victorious, a few real friends, avoid extravagances.

In 12th house, troubles in childhood, bossy, intense in feelings, danger of injury, scandal, loss of reputation from opposition. Liability of imprisonment. Mars in Libra or Pisces indicates poverty, misfortune, secret enemies, defective eyesight and death in seclusion or restraint.

Mars-Saturn Conjunction

This is a very precarious conjunction. Usually it is not harmonious. One undergoes hardship and danger. A man of strong determination. No deviation from selected path. Suffers financial loss through brothers. Conquers enemies, is argumentative, without any peace of mind. Thievish and war-like nature. If conjunction is in 3rd, 6th, or 10th house one will be like a king, loved by all and be famous.

This conjunction is termed as accident-prone. When favourable in 1st, gain through in-laws, and from journeys. In 2nd, wealth after marriage. In 4th, gain of wealth. In 5th, wealth after birth of son. In 7th gain through opposite sex, comforts from wife and children. In 8th troubles. In 9th gain, power etc. after performing religious ceremony of his elders. In 12th house good results are indicated.

But when afflicted, overall results are loss of wealth, death by accident, loss through dacoits etc.

5. Jupiter

Jupiter is significator of children, education, religion, prosperity, fame, gain, good marital order. Providential help, political power, good luck, finances and long journeys, etc.

When Jupiter is malefic by ownership of houses or afflicted, indicates extremists, is liberal, lavish, extravagant, careless, over-optimistic; disputes, gambles, law suits, disagreements, contentions and unpopular etc.

In 1st house, one is fortunate, long life, happy, blessed with children, fearless, faithful, sincere, generous, executive with power and authority. One will lead position in life in social, business, educational circles. Also denotes high standing like judge, banker, doctor, Government officer, etc.

But if debilitated in Ascendant reverse results.

In 2nd house, general prosperity, wealth, success and great riches. Blessed with power and authority. Gain through Government Law, insurance, education and literature.

In 3rd house, benefits through brothers, education, writings, publication, literature and travelling. Cheerful, good in speech, popular, fame and good education.

In 4th house, gain and happiness in family life. Overcome difficulties. Will acquire property. Fortunate, good wife, food and conveyance.

In 5th house, good luck, children, entertainment of high order, through love and opposite sex. Dutiful and prosperous children. Learned, charming etc.

In 6th house, gain and profits through service, favour and gain through subordinates and servants, cheerful, victory over enemies, gain through politicians.

In 7th house, spouse of good understanding. Gain and success through marriage; good, amiable, learned. Gain in partnership, litigation and legal affairs.

In 8th house, favourable for study of occult subjects, has peaceful and natural death. Gain through marriage, inheritance etc.

In 9th house, helps to acquire a unique position. Religious, has providential help. Zealous, has broad outlook and thoughts. Helpful to others. Prophetic dreams. Gain from publication and foreign travel. Good children.

In 10th house, outstanding position in life, fame, power, authority, high position, all round prosperity. Wealthy, gain through good contacts of V.I.Ps., etc.

In 11th house, gains through persons in authority, is wealthy, famous and gets honour. Good position and gain through connections. Good position in life.

In 12th house, it renders success in hospitals, public institutions etc. Success over troubles and enemies. Peculiar experiences with love, affection and religion.

Note: Malefic Jupiter reduces above results. It is not considered auspicious for Taurus, Libra and Capricorn Ascendants.

6. Venus

Venus is the planet of love and beauty, signifies harmony, union, life partner, vehicle, ornaments, sex appeal, business, happiness and well-being. Also signifies beauty, modesty, virtue, sincerity, artistic disposition, conjugal happiness, refined and polished nature. Relations with opposite sex, attraction, love, passions and generosity, etc.

In 1st house indicates good personality, social status, love of worldly pleasures, luxury, amusements and enjoyments. Influence of opposite sex and gain through that. Money through music, dance, cinema, paintings, fine arts, etc.

In 2nd house, good for finances, greedy, eyes lustrous. Excellent for singers. Goodwill and favour from others. Sociable and loved by all.

In 3rd house, strong liking for fine arts, poetry, good mental development, good relations with brothers and sisters. Refined nature, creative, etc.

In 4th house, favourable to domestic affairs, well furnished house, good conveyance, love of home, popular in public and acquisition of house, property if favourably aspected by Sun, Moon or Jupiter.

In 5th house, creates interest in love affairs, has lovely children and gains through them. Idealistic love relations, good marriage and gain through speculation, investment and amusement projects. Success through social life.

In 6th house, victory over enemies, good health, gain in

employment from employer. Care needed while eating and drinking. Love of pets and small animals.

In 7th house, indicates happy and romantic married life, love, affection, gain by marriage, success in public relations. Enjoyment and happiness. Wealthy and prosperous. Clever in coition.

In 8th house, luck and gain through partner and inheritance. Peaceful natural death, rich, good position. Cordial relations with all. Interest in the psychic.

In 9th house, creates opportunities for travel and gains abroad. Optimistic, intelligent, royal favour, prosperous, fond of fine arts.

In 10th house, one becomes popular in public life. Renowned, wealthy, gain through women, happy domestic life. Loved by opposite sex.

In 11th house, denotes universal brotherhood. Learned, wise, fond of company of opposite sex, good social contacts, popular.

In 12th house, indicates secret love affairs, pleasures of beds, excessive greed for money. Inclined to romance, wealthy, affection for others.

Cancer, Scorpio, Capricorn are the worst signs for Venus in 12th house; indicates ardent desire for physical and emotional pleasures, with others, detrimental due to excesses. Ladies are society whores and men may maintain brothels etc. or have illicit relations with many women.

Conjunctions

Sun-Venus conjunction shows a warm hearted and affectionate nature. Fond of fine arts. Relations with opposite sex. Gain through women.

Mars-Venus is an important conjunction. The native will be rash, sexy, under influence of opposite sex, obstinate and victorious over enemies. It creates immoral tendencies because Venus stands for sex and Mars infuses an animal spirit and heat and native may act suddenly, emotionally, dramatically and spontaneously. One will be attached to another person's wife or husband. Such natives are sex-ridden unless controlled by Saturn.

7. Saturn

The mighty Saturn is more a friend than a foe. Is an impartial hard task-master, serious and conservative. Signifies longevity, makes one careful, thoughtful, laborious, violent, envious, accumulator of wealth, prudent, contemplative, reserved, economical, patient.

When afflicted, is melancholic, deceitful, avaricious, impotent, secretive, suspicious, laborious, pessimistic. It is a planet of restrictions and limitations. It creates friendship with wicked persons

Saturn gives pleasures, wealth, fame, position, success and also reverse of above. It has trait of "Distributive Justice".

Its transit over the natal planets is of great importance.

In 1st house, Saturn indicates a melancholy mind, evil thoughts, struggle in work, and if well placed indicates royal qualities, power, position, diplomacy, independent thinker, practical and intellectual.

In 2nd house, maximum labour, minimum wages. Struggle, harsh speech, business loss, unpopular, fond of drinking, weak eyesight, etc.

In 3rd house, indicates increase in income, gains wealth, death of brother, victory over enemies, cautious, less peace of mind, wise and valorous.

In 4th house, impairs family happiness. Sudden losses, success in foreign land, loss of ancestral property, licentious scandal, less happiness.

In 5th house, abortive tendencies, suffers for want of a son. Disappointment in love affairs and loss in speculation. Royal disfavour, etc.

In 6th house, makes one adamant, victorious over enemies, if strong. Labour troubles. Increase in income, popular, great authority but troubles.

In 7th house, unhappy, delayed marriage. Humiliation due to women. Not wealthy. Diplomat, political success. Travels much, foreign honour, etc.

In 8th house, struggles, fond of several women, long life, criminal acts, loss of health, weak eyesight, disappointments, opposition from family.

In 9th house, legal success, founder of charitable institutions, scientific mind. If planet is strong, will be wealthy, charitable, religious and brings easy money.

In 10th house, rise in life, speedy promotions, sudden reversals and downfall, patience, firmness. Invariably it is not good but if yogakarka exalted etc. will bestow good results.

In 11th house, one is learned, respected, very wealthy, much landed property, broken education, conveyance, political success, ambitious yet frustrated.

In 12th house it creates secret enemies, secluded life, danger of imprisonment, downfall, losses, accident, injury, dissatisfaction in sexual life, etc.

8. Rahu and Ketu

Rahu and Ketu are termed as shadowy planets and are also known as Dragon's head and Dragon's tail. Rahu denotes Saturn and Ketu denotes Mars.

Rahu and Ketu indicate love affairs, evil thoughts, dissatisfaction, fear complex, harsh speech, illegal cohabitation, pilgrimage, denial of progeny and adoption of child. Defective eyesight, delay, impediments, change of residence, wicked temperament. Financial gain, jewellery and Government position, etc.

Rahu in Houses

Rahu in 1st house or Ascendant indicates honour, wealth, favour through religious, educational or scientific affairs. It adds power to the personality but one does malicious deeds and is fond of opposite sex.

In 2nd house, indicates fortune through heritance or gain by legacy or gifts, also by science and learning. Opposes others. Danger or assault from enemies.

In 3rd house, one has interest in spiritual and educational matters. Gain through brothers, neighbours, journeys, writings or publishing. Proud, courageous, optimistic. One attains good fortune and long life.

Rahu in 4th house denotes gain by property and in an unexpected manner. Long life and is trustworthy. Hard hearted, worried but when in Aries, Taurus, Gemini or Virgo denotes gain from the Government.

Rahu in 5th house frees the native from many troubles. Son late in life, disturbed peace of mind. One gains public office and favour.

In 6th house valorous and long-lived but oppressed by enemies, he however has victory over them. Faithful and honest. Gain through service.

In 7th house, one is self-willed and independent. A wise partner. In male chart, adverse for virility. Impairs conjugal happiness. No peace of mind. One has illegal contacts with opposite sex.

In 8th house, promotes health and longevity. Evil for mental aptitude, unholy acts, inclined to much sex, a few sons, earns name, fame but blemished. Financial condition is mixed, oppressed by enemies.

In 9th house, success in education, favourable for foreign travel, true dreams and prophetic actions, intelligence, opposed to father. He has name, fame and wealth. No gain from father. An excellent position.

In 10th house, one achieves honour, credit and high position by merit of hard work and ability. Proud and fearless. Powerful enemies and not reliable friends. A few sons. Liaison with opposite sex.

In 11th house, the native is wealthy and long-lived. Meritorious, intelligent, a few sons, travels, famous, health is generally good.

In 12th house, gain by secret methods or in seclusion. Success in occultism. Adverse for health, initially frustrated but comes out successful. Courageous, unfavourable for pleasures of bed.

Ketu in Houses

In 1st house, the native is devoid of happiness, denotes loss and scandal. Afflicted health of eyes and face. Avaricious, worried. Domestic happiness is impaired. But Ketu here in Capricorn or Aquarius is benefic.

In 2nd house, misfortune in finances, loss to property, fear and worries.

In 3rd house, gives mental anxiety, is intelligent, has unfavourable journeys. Loss of brother. Long life but wound on arm is indicated. Courageous.

In 4th house, family discord. Loss of ancestral property. Malicious.

In 5th house, denial or shortage of children and little happiness from them.

In 6th house, afflicted health, many enemies but one will overpower them. Danger from reptiles or animals. Famous, fixed views, childhood not happy.

In 7th house, troubled married life, sick wife, may cause separation, illegal connections with opposite sex, adultrous, worried, loss of vitality.

In 8th house, loss through fraud, sudden or violent death. Wounds, separation from dear ones. One has desire for other's property and wives.

In 9th house, unfortunate travels and imprisonment in foreign land. Wealthy, pilgrimage indicated, religious, but worried. Proud, courageous, intelligent and a hypocrite.

In 10th house, loss to position by deception and adverse public conditions. One is against father. Courageous, intelligent, shrewd, accidents from conveyance, is wealthy.

In 11th house, undesirable association, false friends. Wealthy, popular, good authority, gain, and success. Good deeds. Few sons and worries from them.

In 12th house, loss and troubles through secret enemies. Afflicted health, is secretive. Sinful deeds and licentious. Eye disease. Weak and victorious in disputes.

Note: The results of planets in different houses as enumerated above are not firm. The same be modified according to the sign they are posited in and the aspects the planet receive alongwith conjunction and transit of other planets etc.

ASPECTS

Aspect can be defined as the angular distance between planets. It can be good or bad. In Hindu astrology all planets aspect to 7th house from their position. In addition Jupiter, Rahu and Ketu have 5th and 9th aspects. Mars has 4th and 8th aspects whereas Saturn has 3rd and 10th aspects.

The opposition aspect becomes extremely good in Hindu astrology when it is produced by Jupiter and Moon. A planet aspecting its own house, exalted house increases the signification of that house.

We describe only the fundamentals of main aspects in brief. For details refer to the author's other world-famous books.

1. *Conjunction*

It is a first house aspect (Zero degree). When two or more planets are in one house, they are in conjunction. They can be good or evil according to the ownership of houses, their natural qualities like benefic or malefic, including aspects on the conjunction. Conjunction of lords 1, 4, 7 and 10 houses and trine aspect (9th and 5th house aspect) when unassociated with lords of other houses are not only powerful in producing good effects of signification of houses located and owned by them, but brings honour, wealth and general prosperity even if located in evil houses. But these very lords, if very powerful and strong by position, in own sign, or in exaltation, regardless of other sources of evils, such as their union with evil house lord, become not only powerful to do good, but help other planets associated with them towards the same object.

Conjunction of trine lords (5th, 9th houses) are always good irrespective of their location but when these lords are associated with lords of 8th or 12th house, success is endangered.

2. *Sextile*

It is 3rd and 11th house Hindu aspect. It is termed a benefic aspect of 60 degrees. This aspect contains the potentiality of the future. You can take initiative during this aspect. An easy aspect and reinforces the weak points.

3. *Trine*

It is 5th and 9th house Hindu aspect. It includes creative flow of life, energies that allow for easy expression. It is a strong benefic of 120 degrees. A fortunate aspect for harmony, peace and does much to improve adverse aspect. When occurring between Sun and Moon it is more fortunate than any other aspect.

4. *Square*

It is 4th and 10th Hindu aspect. It indicates challenges from circumstances, a time for new initiatives and action in forward motion. A strong malefic aspect of 90 degrees of *Nature of Saturn*. Most critical and conflicting aspect. It gives disturbed, prejudiced, or adverse conditions and circumstances accompanying it. A separative aspect. Indicates angle of pain and sorrow, perturbed peace of mind, worry, anxiety and despondency. The effect of this aspect turns the tide of fortune.

5. *Opposition*

This is 7th house or 180 degrees aspect. A malefic aspect of perfect balance. This aspect includes confrontation and partnership. A time for confrontation with others. Change of circumstances.

Except Jupiter, all other aspects of opposition are termed malefic.

Significator for Houses

The "Significator" or Karka of house is a planet which is held to signify a person or event. The planet governing the Ascendant is termed as native's significator. For example, 7th house lord is the significator of his wife or partner. Beside these planets, there are Karkas for each house also. In the table below we provide Karka or Significator for each house, which can be memorised.

House	Karka	House	Karka
I	Sun	VII	Venus
II	Jupiter	VIII	Saturn
III	Mars	IX	Jupiter
IV	Moon	X	Mercury
V	Jupiter	XI	Jupiter
VI	Mars	XII	Saturn

3

YOUR BASIC NATURE

Before starting this and the subsequent chapters, you must know your Ascendant or Lagna, so that you can follow them correctly.

You must have your horoscope drawn as per Hindu system and from there remember your Ascendant; or

Consult the Table of Ascendants provided in this book. It is easy to find your Ascendant with your birth data from that according to the method given in the Table.

The characteristics of each sign are discussed from this chapter onward. If the Ascendant Lord is posited unafflicted in the Ascendant, it will manifest the results. Malefic planets posited in Lagna or aspect Lagna will change the results and be modified accordingly.

1. Aries or Mesha

Physical Appearance

Persons born under this sign possess lean and muscular body, middle stature neither thick nor stout, ruddy complexion, long face and neck. Broad head at temples and narrow at chin. Thin features, mark or scar on head or temples. Bushy eyebrows. Eyes are grey to greyish brown.

Mental Tendencies

Ambitious, dominating, active, energetic, courageous and lover of independence. Rash and aggressive.

Personality

Male: Simple, frank and outspoken. Capable of holding command in executive position. Not good in organising schemes but can implement them nicely. Lover of independence, brave, zealous, dogmatic views and can make quick decisions. Life will be full of struggle and fortune is variable, strained family ties, few children, changes residence, victory over many enemies, a good mechanical ability. Good health.

Female: Truthful, quarrelsome, energetic, has red tinge on the face. Independent views. She always speaks highly of her family. Jealous and proud. She expects to be praised by her husband but cannot tolerate that her husband should praise any other lady in her presence. Aggressive, very romantic, she only loves the person whom she can admire. Such ladies are brave, generous, diplomatic and of dogmatic views. They marry early and in a hurry. Quick, fiery and of rash temperament. Cannot tolerate any neglect by her partner. Such career girls can handle any profession. A good housewife too. She demands a lot from her partner and returns with twice that. They normally enjoy good health. Generally Arian ladies overpower their husbands which should be avoided.

Arian husbands are very desirable partners. Usually they select beautiful, clever and good wives. Generous and bountiful, romantic but spendthrift. Rash and passionate.

Traits to be Corrected

Arians should avoid rash temperament, too much of independence of views. Should not be dogmatic in their opinion but listen to others. They should be of adjustable nature.

2. Taurus or Rishba

Physical Appearance

Taurus-born persons (both sexes) are of short to middle stature, broad forehead, bright eyes, thick and stout neck, dark hair, clear complexion, well developed body.

Mental Tendencies

Persevering, constant, conservative, determined, obstinate, ambitious for power, yet social, affectionate and loving but can also be very reasonable and prejudiced. When angry will not stop at anything. Slow but good steady worker.

Personality

Male: Such persons are enduring, very patient, violent and unrelenting. They should think before they act. When opposed can become stubborn and unyielding. Sincere, reliable and trustworthy.

They are fond of love, pleasures, natural beauty, art, music and literature. Fond of ease, comforts, opposite sex and will have many love affairs. They enjoy a good health. Divorce is rare with them. Cooperative and love domestic life.

Female: Taurus-born ladies are practical, become furious and violent when severely angered. Secretive and reserved. They are reliable, trustworthy and sincere. Agreeable in nature, obedient, good hostesses and keep the house tidy and modern. Reserved and calm. Such ladies should not doubt the character of their husbands. Anxious for a harmonious wedded life. Intellectual and constant in love. Fond of music and art. Not so demanding except in love and loyalty. Good mothers too. They expect care from their husbands in all respects. A dependable and predictable lady.

Husbands: Taurus husbands are devoted to their wives and adore them. Reliable, generous and faithful. They never neglect the house and the needs of the partner. The husband likes to see his wife well dressed, attractive and pleasing. Cooperative in domestic life.

Traits to be Corrected

They should not be obstinate, not slow in action, not be selfish and vindictive. They should not retain anger for a long time. Avoid doubting others.

3. Gemini or Mithun

Physical Appearance

Geminians are tall, upright, slender, quick, thin legs and visible veins. Moderate complexion, long arms, face, nose and chin. Hazel or grey eyes and look sharp, active and quick.

Mental Tendencies

Learning and good education. Lovely and quick witted, intelligent, nervous and restless. Fond of fine arts.

Geminian ladies are very difficult to understand, being of dual nature, but very reliable in emergency. Good education. Such damsels are witty, intelligent, lovely but nervous and restless. Fond of music, dance, painting, travels and inventions. Science subject will suit them best.

Personality

Males: Such persons lack in concentration and quick decision. They are ambitious, aspiring, curious to know the results of their efforts immediately. Argumentative. Work systematically. Fond of mental recreations. At times restless, anxious, highly strung and diffusive. Want love, change and diversity in all spheres of life. Good advisors and reliable. Progressive, energetic, refuse to bide by rules. Will face lot of changes in life. Enjoys the life to maximum and also suffers continuous misfortunes. The more the romance, the happier they will be.

Females: Geminian ladies are very intelligent, and want mental companionship. After marriage will not give up outside activities. Lack of concentration and quick decision. Argumentative (to be avoided). Good advisors and reliable. Want change in all walks of life. Cannot be imposed upon quickly. Such ladies have influence on opposite sex. Fault-finding nature, so cannot make permanent selections. Of dual nature. Such ladies need pity and not anger. True in love, good mothers.

Traits to be Corrected

Geminians should avoid worry and anxiety. Be cautious to avoid strifes, not hasty. Events will be faster in their life than others, so they should bear them and not feel disheartened. Cultivate physical and mental poise.

4. Cancer or Karaka

Physical Appearance

Cancer-born persons are not usually above average height. Tendency to stoutness. Short nose, grey or light blue eyes. Ladies have round face, full cheeks, nose prominent at the tip. Pale complexion sometimes very beautiful. Wide breasts, small hands and feet.

Mental Tendencies

Cancerians are fond of change, novelty and travelling. Attached to relations and home, inclined to public life, sympathetic, changeful and impatient. Emotional and over-sensitive. Diplomatic, discreet and conventional. Anger comes and goes quickly.

Personality

Males: Changeable, ups and downs of positions and occupations, of fertile imagination, sentimental and talkative. They face physical danger but are brave. Emotional and conventional. Such persons have strong emotional and romantic nature. Fickle-minded, secretive, impressionable and magnetic. Commercial careers suit them best, cannot tolerate dishonesty. Devoted to domestic life and can sacrifice all for their children, they prefer to marry a homely girl. Criticising and interfering in household matters causes unpleasant atmosphere.

Females: Cancerian damsels are sincere, loyal, affectionate, dutiful and devoted to their husbands. Good mothers, moody but adaptable to family atmosphere. Changeable in nature. Secretive, sensitive, romantic and imaginative. Easily influenced, emotional and hospitable. Impressionable and magnetic, careful for their tenacity and honour. Love only the persons whom they like the most. Such ladies can be quiet, touchy and not so jealous. Patience is their loveliest virtue. They are more interested in getting small money from many sources than a big amount from one source. Economical, tolerable, in case of adverse circumstances they only shed tears.

Traits to be Corrected

In spite of all good points as above, they should be patient, enduring, and avoid sensitiveness. They should avoid inferiority complex and not be over-anxious, lazy and passive. Indolence and changeability are their weak points to be corrected. Cancerians should not be vindictive and should control their passions. Cancerians must overcome their timid nature.

5. Leo or Simha

Physical Appearance

Leonians have broad shoulders, ruddy and florid complexion, large bones and muscles. Tall, upright body, better formed than lower portion. Thin waist, prominent knees. Big and round head. Majestic appearance, imposing, commanding and dignified. Attractive and large staring eyes. In short, a royal disposition.

Leo ladies in addition are introverts, energetic, gregarious and beautifully indolent. Blush on their face, they walk straight with proudly hidden quivering intensity. Some eyes are blue but generally they have dark brown eyes that are soft, gentle, then snap and crackle with fire, hair is dark, commanding air and stately personality.

Mental Tendencies

Ambitious, generous, honourable, frank, warm-hearted, self-confident, fearless, impulsive, determined, persevering and fond of power and distinctions. Liking for art, cheerful, optimistic disposition. Magnanimous and generous. Large-hearted and noble but harsh in temperament.

Personality

Males: Good natured, frank, outspoken, strong-willed, independent, forceful and impulsive. Helpful to mankind, of wise judgement. Very independent in views and of rash temperament, have excellent organising capacity. Constructive, practical, inventive and impressionable. They make their presence felt. Leaders, have vitality and vigour. Brave, constant in love. Generally teased by opponents whom they face up to bravely. Liberal views, generally have robust health.

Females: Leo ladies are ridiculously popular, born to rule and to dictate to others. A man who expects a Leo girl to worship at his feet is living in a fool's paradise. Leonians manage their homes in an excellent way. Self-sacrificing and have everlasting love. Leo ladies should not doubt their Leo husbands for being popular with the opposite sex. They need one to keep them under their control. Unselfish, very passionate, dogmatic ideas, Leonians should not think that their word should be law at home or outside. They accept gifts smilingly, can be flattered. Leos are athletes and fond of sports. Such ladies can be arrogant, truthful, witty, strong in body and a free bird as they cannot be confined within the four walls of the house.

Traits to be Corrected

Since Leonians are determined and of dogmatic views, they should listen to others. Their roaring like a lion lands them in trouble which should be avoided. Arguments, altercations and actions annoying others should be avoided. Leonians must avoid forcing their views, desires upon others. They should not be arrogant, should restrict their wants and be economical. Should save for old age. They should not be carried away by others' flattery. Avoid rash temperament and remain more detached from feelings.

6. Virgo or Kanya

Physical Appearance

Virgo natives are tall with slender bodies. Dark hair, curved and hairly eyebrows, thin and shrill voice and walk quickly. Straight nose, appear younger than their age, a pronounced forehead. Frank and honest expression of the eyes and sometimes beautiful blue eyes.

The eyes of Virgo-born ladies so very clear that you can see your reflection therein. Delicate ears, nose and lips.

Mental Tendencies

Fond of learning, active mind, good mental abilities and critical. Methodical, nervous and lacking in self-confidence. Perceptive and somewhat intuitive. Keeps things orderly and thinks in a methodical way. A deep thinker. Uncomfortable in crowds but likes seclusion. Fastidious and exacting in working and romance.

Personality

Males: Virgoans are ambitious for wealth. Thoughtful, conservative and industrious. Not easily contended, changeable nature. Often change their residence. They have commercial instinct, are practical, methodical and discriminative. Experts in finding faults with others. Love details of things, cautious about their own interests. Speculative nature. Fond of study of science particularly about medicine, food, diet, hygiene etc. Many ups and downs in life. They have wanderlust, peaceful domestic life. Religious and God-fearing wife. In love affairs, hardly succeed due to fault-finding nature. After marriage home bird, limited good children.

Females: In addition to the above traits, ladies are accommodating and adjustable. Saving nature. Happy married life. Sex is a mean idea with them whereas they enjoy the company of the opposite sex. Fond of study. Sincere in love. Shy, obstacles in life will not deter them . In case they find some flaws or imperfections in love or marriage, will not hesitate to break the relations, otherwise supreme in love. Delicacy in romance is their weakness. When annoyed they can be shrewd and fussy. Virgo ladies are nobody's fools. Such ladies can be won over with grace and taste and not by physical charms as in the case of Leo ladies.

Traits to be Corrected

They should not be sensitive, sarcastic and chatty. Fault-finding habit should be avoided; also should not be revengeful. They should be careful with their friends and servants who may betray them of secrets, exploit them and may take them to court to spoil their reputation. They should avoid alcohol and drugs, instead use vegetarian diet.

7. Libra or Tula

Physical Appearance

Good complexion, well-formed body, tall, slender in youth but tendency to stoutness in middle age. Brown to black hair. Blue or brown eyes. Passionate, oval face, parrot-like nose. Curves and contours of body are regular. Often dimples. Almond eyes which speak for themselves. Good looking, graceful and youthful appearance, sweet smiles and attractive countenance.

Libra ladies are the emblem of beauty, look like dolls. Well-formed body, passionate, forceful laughter, charming expressions, graceful, magnetic and almond-like speaking eyes.

Mental Tendencies

Librans are fond of dress, perfumes, art and music. Fertile imagination and correct intuition, brilliant, intellectual, considerate, admirable, refined and pleasant. Cheerful, fond of society and amusement and under influence of opposite sex. Diplomatic, fond of lovely things, argumentative and of materialistic nature.

Personality

Males: Librans are courteous and hospitable. Fond of beauty in all forms, easily appeased. Always enjoy the company of the opposite sex. Affectionate, kind, compassionate and impressionable. Fond of opposite sex. They have warmth and charming manners. They are fond of conjugal affection. Full of charms and manners. They enjoy happy family life generally. Honest in love and have everlasting friends, sincere and expert in love affairs. They marry early, happy at home and in social life. They have a limited number of children.

Females: The beautiful Libra damsels are very courteous, hospitable, fond of beauty in all forms, usually smart, easily appeased, affectionate and kind. Impressionable, sexy, passionate and of commanding nature. Warm and charming manners. Popular in life. Full of charms and manners. Without friends, Libra ladies cannot pass time and are not satisfied. Of adjustable nature and do not seek divorce. They are unconventional but their sweet manners, smiles, and smooth ability will be helpful to their spouse even during any crisis or family problem. Good mothers of limited good and talented children. In the house, they will reign. Their husbands are lucky and are to be congratulated for having partners like them, O, Libra damsels!

Traits to be Corrected

Librans should control their emotional nature and avoid spending much on luxuries. Being social, sexy and passionate, they should see that people do not take undue advantage of them. They should be decisive, avoid copying others. They should learn to say "No" to people in spite of the fact that they are liberal and generous. Librans should forgive if not forget. Avoid arguments and bossing over others.

8. Scorpio or Varischak

Physical Appearance

Scorpions have good personality, well-proportioned body, long hands, good stature, broad face, commanding appearance. Tendency to stoutness, prominent brows and dusky complexion. Such persons have a tinge of redness on their faces.

Mental Tendencies

This sign represents the poisonous Scorpion. This sign represents two types, the higher or the lower, the former has control over their senses, the latter are jealous of others, rude, strong-willed and of terrorising tendencies. Reliant, bold, fixed views, lose their temper quickly, get irritated and are highly sexed. They have rational thinking, hate gossips, are frank and sarcastic. Cunning but very true, loyal, faithful and reliable, when higher side prevails, otherwise the opposite. They should not work under pressure. They are impulsive, courageous, hard to influence and critical.

Personality

   Male: Scorpions cannot remain idle. While facing obstacles and hindrances, they are at their best and never surrender but fight to end. Of fertile imagination, tenacious, determined and quick-witted. Alert, forceful and positive. Often blunt, fond of contest and travel. They are impulsive, forceful, have constructive and destructive ability, they can be frugal and economical, unyielding and self-made nature. Sometimes they get ill-reputed. A subtle mind hard to influence, not easily imposed upon. Scorpions are interested in occult, chemical research and mystery. Self-assertion, an extremist, have strong likes and dislikes and have tendency to override and keep others under control. They enjoy life from highest pleasure to lowest tone. Lucky in finance and worldly articles. They are good friends as well as worst enemies, so life-long friendship for them is not possible.

Females: Scorpion ladies enjoy the life if the partners are equally of genuine affection and deep love. Adjustable nature and know how to please their husbands. These ladies are no doubt hard workers, they suddenly lose their temper, forget themselves and pounce upon their husbands or on others regardless of their positions. They are very passionate and sexy and fond of the opposite sex. Such ladies are not soft or naive. One cannot see their emotions which are not reflected on their faces. They are magnetic, proud and totally confident. They want less restrictions but more opportunities. Cannot sit idle. They should not be insulted openly as they will hide their power of retaliation with a smile, and will strike latter. They can be overbearing, domineering, sarcastic and frigid, then turn as hot as an oven. They hate with bitterness and love with fierce abandon. They want a male who can control them and make them proud. They are human X-ray machines, so do not flirt with them, but instead be true in romance and other dealings.

Traits to be Corrected

Scorpions should not be sarcastic, over critical, should control their temper, try to avoid secret enmity, and not be selfish. They should be patient and watch for results of their efforts. They should not be of revengeful nature or fall prey to the habit of drinking.

If the lower side of Scorpio sign operates, then they are masters in creating anarchy, lawlessness, and destructions as they are social firebrands and dangerous to community.

9. Sagittarius or Dhanu

Physical Appearance

A well proportioned and well developed body. Tall, slender, generally long and oval face, large forehead, high or bushy eyebrows, long nose, bright expressive blue or hazel eyes. Clear complexion, charming appearance, graceful look and handsome figure. Double chin, open and cheerful features inviting friendship and exchange of ideas. ,

Mental Tendencies

Such persons are generous, restless, bold, good hearted, pushful, ambitious but greedy and aspiring, good tempered, frank, free, cheerful, charitable and friendly. They look to the bright side of things, dauntless with self-confidence. Active, sympathetic and somewhat impulsive. Fond of travelling and speed, fast cars, aeroplanes, and drive the vehicles magnetically. Also fond of voyages, outdoor sports and exercises. Blessed with energy to face obstacles. Sagittarians are inclined to philosophy, law, medicine or religion.

Personality

Males: Sagittarians are not timid, will not fear and trembie in adverse circumstances. They act after deep consideration, are jovial, generous and charitable. Love liberty, independence and freedom. Frank, fearless, demonstrative, outspoken, ambitious, sincere and quick. God-fearing and religious. Respect religion, law and order and customs. Fond of higher education. Sagittarian males flare up quickly which last for a short time. Fond of games, clubs and sports as these are more important to them than their family life. Sagittarians are persons of morality and dignity, maturity comes late in life. They should not develop hatred towards their brothers and parents, this will not pay them. They will be generous towards the opposite sex and friendly with them. At home Sagittarians may not be independent which they desire, so they should be of adjustable nature.

Females: In addition to the above such ladies are fond of home, will not interfere in their husbands' affairs. They will not suggest unless asked for and are of adjustable nature. Such ladies are liked by their friends and are generous towards the opposite sex. Their nature can melt the hardest hearts. They like sumptuous food, wine, good and nice clothes. Extravagant by nature. Sagittarians have casual behaviour towards romance and marriage, misleading one to think they are lacking in sentiments; no doubt it is wrong, then why give such impressions to others? A lovely hostess and cook. Such ladies entertain more graciously the guests at home. Their loyalty, trust and affection are for their partner and friends which do not make them tied down. An incurable idealist.

Traits to be Corrected

Sagittarians should be moderate and not hate their relations, parents and brothers. Exaggeration and continuous speech without truth, false promises, insults or hurting others are their basic traits, which should be avoided. Care for the family in addition to outdoor activities. Should not be of vindictive mind. They disturb the people in unnecessary ways and change their opinion often, which need correction.

10.Capricorn or Makar

Physical Appearance

Prominent features, usually thin and long or prominent nose, black hair, thin beard, becomes tall after 16 years of age. There will be scar on knee cap or a mole.

Capricornian ladies are thin, wiry and soft. Such ladies have straight, lank, dark hair, dark steady eyes, and swarthy olive or tan complexion. Often eyes are blue. Many of them have strong feet and wear sensible shoes and have sensible skin and do not wear much make-up. Lots of them are allergic to make-up. Naturally, they have natural beauty giving them lovely complexion, firm features and bright eyes.

Mental Tendencies

They are economical, prudent, self-willed, reserved, pensive, reasonable, thoughtful and of practical nature. Calculative and businesslike. Secretive, quiet, much mental ingenuity and fertility, changeable capracious and will have push and confidence. Desirous of wealth, power, and authority, methodical and plodding.

Personality

Males: They have special organising capacity with good tolerance, patience and steady nature. Serious, quiet, thoughtful, contemplative, possessing dignity and self-esteem. Also, they are cautious, hard workers, capable of much endeavour. They do not depend on hopes of others. Not demonstrative in feelings and do not readily show their sympathy. It is not easy to cheat Capricornians. Make permanent relations after test. Such people are reliant, thrifty, respectful to religion. They will rise gradually, will make repeated attempts and finally succeed. They will use everything and every method for a material purpose. They are not romantic. Choosy about partner. Less real friends, slow in passion and afraid to proceed unless they obtain consent thrice and in a sure way. They provide all facilities to their family slowly.

Females: Many Capricornian ladies are career girls to whom love and marriage is a second choice. They want respect, security, authority and position. Such ladies are ultra-feminine, can be flirtatious and charming enough to make a man feel like a giant grizzly bear who can protect them. They have a steady determination to snag the right man, who can become important, make them proud. They will execute any work quickly after taking careful decision. These damsels have special organising capacity with good tolerance, patience and steady nature. They are happier with men with good position, security and good financial position. They will not pin their hopes on others and are not demonstrative in love. They will rise gradually, steady in emotions and romance. They are subjected to many moods, are as firm as a rock. They cannot accept teasing lightly, so keep it to a minimum.

Traits to be Corrected

They should avoid nervousness and discontentment but develop dignity, diplomacy, avoid selfishness, egoism and pessimism. They should not become desperate and broken-hearted. Capricornians should not overtax themselves but instead take plenty of rest. They must avoid fatigue. Care of health is necessary.

11. Aquarius or Kumbh

Physical Appearance

Persons born under this sign are tall with full stature. Strong, well-formed body and features, clear complexion, oval face, handsome appearance, brown hair, mole or scar on calf muscles. Fleshy face. Good looking and friendly countenance.

Ladies have some magic or mysterious knowledge in their eyes which are dreamy, vague, wandering expression and often blue, green or blue. Handsome appearance. A nobility of profile. Features are finely chiselled. They have drooping heads. Most women of this type are puzzling, lovely with a haunting wistful beauty, but they are changeable. Next to Libra, they are the most beautiful damsels. Their manner of dressing can stop others dead in their tracks, conventional in their costumes. Hair style will be more unusual than others.

Mental Tendencies:

Intelligent, good memory and reasoning faculty. Very capable of dealing with facts, possess good concentration, kind, humane, and self-controlled. Constant, persevering, happy disposition, inventive and psychic. Have many friends. Can read other's character, broad outlook and like solitude.

Personality

Males: Such males are serious, quiet, thoughtful and of contemplative nature. Intelligent, cautious, prudent, economical and practical. Very social but choosy about friends. Have organising capacity. Shrewd, clear-headed, quick-witted and wide awake. Will do things which are morally right. They have their own individuality and speciality. Constant in friendship. Best suited for research work. Aquarians are strong in likes and dislikes. They set examples by doing rather than preaching. Blessed with good family and sound financial position. Aquarians are intelligent, contemplative and carry on research, have little time to attend to wife and family. This may not be taken as their drawback and lack of interest because they are humane, kind, sympathetic, accommodative, generous and a genius.

Females: Aquarian wives are unconventional, they change the partner if not satisfied, otherwise will cooperate to the maximum. They are constant in friendship, extremely adaptable to all forms of society. One can judge them from their dreamy eyes. Without doubt, ladies do not suspect their husbands. Before a damsel is credited, one should consider her lack of passionate jealousy which is due to something more than strength of character. Honour and wealth come to them. Such ladies are neither very much attached to or detached from family. Aquarians may move with intellectuals freely. They prefer permanent and strong attachments, faithful in love but not demonstrative.

Traits to be Corrected

In case of difference with paramour or friends, they should not show jealousy, possessiveness or prejudice, or be critical, stuffy or ultra conservative. They should not be lazy and lethargic. Aquarians should not be worried, gloomy and pessimistic. Should be alert and pushful but not be very rigid towards those whom they dislike.

12. Pisces or Meena

Physical Appearance

Pisceans are generally of short stature, short limbs, full of fleshy face, pale complexion, muscular and spherical shoulders. Big and protruding eyes, soft and silky hair. Wide mouth inclining to corpulence especially in later years.

The ladies' features are elastic and mobile and one will find more dimples than wrinkles. Eyes are liquid, heavy lidded, and full of strange lights. In body they have some extraordinary grace. Such ladies have short limbs and may become plumpy in later years of life.

Mental Tendencies

Quick in understanding, inspirational, easy-going, good natured, changeful, psychic and emotional. Sarcastic. Normally, they follow the path of least resistance. Fond of music, passionate, affectionate and charitable. Sometimes they are secretive, reserved or mysterious in the way of doing things. Philosophical, lead a romantic life.

Personality

Males: Kind, loving, truthful, courteous and hospitable. Restless, helpful and humane. Lack generally in self-confidence, self-esteem, and cannot harm anyone. They are a puzzle to others and even to themselves, cannot be steady, are sweet tempered and social. Led away by fancies and new ideas, polite and modest. Àt times, they become over-anxious. disheartened, indecisive, and lacking in life and energy. Of varying moods, over-liberal, keep hopes on other's promises, rely on friends and suffer at their hands. Addicted to drinks. Love psychic and adult sciences. Pisceans are best suited as poets, musicians, planning commissioners, painters, nurses, teachers, accountants, bankers, actors or liaison workers. Suspicious by nature but romantic.

Females: These damsel blondes are kind, helpful, loving, truthful and courteous. Lacking generally in self-confidence. They shrink from competitions. Such ladies have self-esteem, are most timid and cannot harm anyone. They cannot be steady. Of varying moods, over liberal and have no desire to dominate their husbands. Piscean ladies want to be protected and taken care of properly. Being cosy and calm, they are proud of their partner and never blame them for any loss or problem created by mistake. Soft, dreamy and womanly. They show unbounded generosity. Occasionally sensitive. They adopt beautifully and quietly to conflicting situations. They can be caught by those who know their elusive secrets. They become deceptive, dreamy and vague at times. Terribly sentimental but on the other side gloomy and feel unequipped to survive. So they should overcome their timidity and doubts.

Traits to be Corrected

Pisceans should not rely too much on their friends, but be choosy about them. A few friends will be sincere, outwardly honest but inwardly scoundrels, cheats and selfish. They should avoid being suspicious and of varying moods. They should cultivate push, be generous but not be over liberal. They should not rely on other's promises or be contemplating and dreaming always.

4

SPOUSES AND MARRIED LIFE

Tennyson has rightly said, "Marriages are made in heaven". Marriage is a union of two hearts and souls to the exclusion of the rest of the world, or, a marriage is a lasting union between a male and a female, governed by a mutual contract, open or secret. Legality or otherwise of a union is of a secondary nature and important from the astrology point of view. The native is fortunate if the marriage is completely successful, otherwise life becomes hell.

"A woman must be a genius to create a good husband." Yes, this quotation of Bolzac is quite true. A woman should create an atmosphere of amnesty and cooperation at home with her husband and other family members. On the other hand T. Fuller has advised all bachelors to "keep the eyes wide open before marriage and then half shut afterwards," for a good and smooth conjugal life.

Ladies are made of an altogether peculiar physical fibre with the characteristics of fair complexion, smiling and charming demeanour, sparkling eyes, rosy nails, slim waist, nimble toes, coy looks, melodious voice, pleasant and graceful manners, elegant attire, natural bashfulness etc. No wonder that nature has chosen them for the purpose of procreation, motherhood and rearing the children with care and love. So in view of the above, their problems are different than that of men. Our Maharishis have chosen to treat them through "Stree Jatak or Female Horoscope". This book takes care of their problems astrologically. For more details on ladies readers should refer to author's world-famous book, *Women and Astrology*.

Spouse means husband or wife and in this context, a major role is played at home by the lady. Every male wants that his partner should be beautiful, of amiable nature, educated and wise, so is the case with ladies.

We shall first indicate some astrological rules dealing with the problem.

Beauty

Beauty is a prerequisite and essential for a woman. According to astrology, all even signs, viz., Taurus, Cancer, Virgo, Scorpio, Capricorn and Pisces are considered as female signs and are preferable or Ascendants or Lagna when a girl is born. Gemini and Libra are male signs yet can be grouped under female sign. Venus and Mars are two female planets and they add complexion and beauty to women if they are in proximity or exactly on the Ascendant.

Women born with Virgo or Pisces ascendants with Hast and Rewati nakshatras respectively, are destined to possess lustre and beauty and are able to maintain it without much effort for a pretty long time. Their natural physical functions are most regular, and these help them in maintaining harmony and peace in their homes.

Women born with Taurus (Rohini) and Libra (Vaisakha) on the Ascendant are good looking, love beauty and neatness and are of harmonious nature. As a wife, such a girl is best.

Ladies with Scorpio Ascendant have a spectacular look, besides their eyes are deep and heart-searching, nose is straight. Their beauty is somewhat peculiar. Sex appeal is abnormal. Ladies born with such Ascendants and majority of planets therein play predominantly. They are more or less showy and take pleasure in concealing their defects skilfully.

These are the guidelines which may not be taken as rigid and final. Overall horoscope is to be checked.

In the previous chapter, we have provided more details.

Marriage

In order to predict a legal marriage, first ascertain if one is destined to marry or not, what type of marriage is possible and when. How will the married life be? Such questions are dealt with hereunder and can be checked from the horoscopes

Promised Marriage

The following few combinations out of many are provided:

1. Moon or Venus in fruitful signs and also in the 7th house.
2. Jupiter or Venus occupy 2nd, 7th or 11th house.
3. Jupiter or Venus is conjoined with Moon in 1st, 5th, 10th or 11th house.
4. Moon as well as Venus is not aspected by Saturn and is stronger than Saturn.
5. Lagna and 7th house lords are in 3rd, 5th, 11th house together.
6. Benefics in 2nd, 7th, 11th houses from Lagna and Moon sign and have favourable connections with benefics.
7. Mercury in 7th house and Venus conjoined with 7th house lord.
8. Lord of 7th in 11th house and Venus in 2nd house.
9. Venus in Lagna, and Lord of Lagna in 7th.
10. Benefics in 1st, 2nd or 7th house, or lords of 2nd and 11th house in mutual exchange.
11. 7th house lord is not posited in 6th, 8th or 12th and is aspected by benefics.

No Marriage

1. If any of the three planets Venus, Sun and Moon is aspected by or conjoined with Saturn, or any one of the trio, particularly if Moon is associated with Saturn's Nakshatra, there is no possibility of marriage.
2. When Sun, Moon and 5th lord are in conjunction with or aspected by Saturn.
3. If Venus is placed at a distance of 43° or more from debilitated Sun and is aspected or conjoined with Saturn, negotiations will fall through at the time of the final stage.
4. If 7th house is vacant and Moon in case of female and Sun in case of man are aspected by Saturn occupying Scorpio sign, marriage is not a certainty.
5. If 7th lord, Lagna and Venus fall in barren signs, viz Gemini, Leo, Virgo and Sagittarius.
6. Malefics in 6th, 7th, 8th houses or malefics on both sides of 7th house are unfavourable for marriage.
7. If Saturn is in 7th aspected and conjoined also with malefics.

8. Venus and Moon are in opposition without any benefic aspect.
9. Venus conjunct Moon aspected by Mars and Saturn and 7th house is not aspected by Jupiter or malefics in 1st, 7th, 12th houses.
10. Lord of 7th in 12th without any benefic aspect but receiving malefic aspects of Saturn, Sun and Rahu (separative aspects).

Delayed Marriage

In case of a male, all information about his wife is to be obtained from 7th house, its lord and Venus.

But in case of a female, 7th, 8th, its lords and Mars are to be analysed to check about the husband of a lady.

Sometimes it happens that a promised marriage comes late in life. Due to change in time and circumstances, nowadays marriages of girls are solemnised between 25 and 30 years but in astrology it is termed late marriage. Cases have come to the author where promised marriages have been delayed up to 36 years or even more. Main planets responsible for such delays are Saturn, Venus, Moon, Jupiter and Rahu. A few combinations in this respect are:

1. If Saturn is either in 1st, 3rd, 5th, 7th, 10th house from Lagna or Moon sign and if Saturn does not own beneficial houses.
2. A malefic in 7th house, Saturn, or even Mars in own sign delays marriage.
3. If Mars is in 8th or Rahu in 7th.
4. If Mars and Venus conjoin in 5th, 7th or 9th house both receive evil aspect from Jupiter.
5. If 7th house lord and Jupiter are aspected by Saturn.
6. Malefics in 6th, 8th or 12th house.
7. If Lagna, Moon and Sun are under malefic aspect.
8. When Rahu and Mars are related to 7th house or Venus.
9. When 7th lord is posited in 6th, 2nd, 12th from 7th house, girl's marriage is delayed. This is a powerful yoga for delayed marriage and is further strengthened when a malefic associates with 7th lord or in 7th house.
10. Rahu and Venus in Lagna or in 7th house or Mars and Sun in 7th house with other afflictions cause delay in marriage.

Time of Marriage

Predicting time of marriage is a ticklish question, which worries the parents about their wards. In such cases the astrologer should check yogas that confer marriage, planetary conditions at birth and in transit, dasa, bhukti and antra dasa etc. He should give due regard to the following points also: (We provide a few yogas and rules in this context)

1. If Ascendant rasi of a Navamsa chart falls in 7th house of birth chart, and 7th lord is in 12th from Ascendant, marriage will take place between 16 and 20 years of age.
2. If 2nd lord is posited in 11th house and 11th lord in 2nd, marriage will be between 16 and 25 years of age.
3. When 2nd lord is in 11th and Lagna lord is in 10th house, marriage may occur between 17 and 20 years of age.
4. When Venus is in Kendra (1,4,7,10) and 7th lord is posited in any house owned by Saturn, aspected by a benefic, marriage age is 23 to 28 years.
5. When 2nd house is occupied by Venus and 7th lord is in 11th house, marriage is between 23 and 28 years of age.
6. When 7th house is occupied by Venus, Moon and Saturn, the marriage will not be possible before 30 years of age. It may be the 35th year also.
7. If Sun is in 7th, and 7th lord conjoins Venus in Kendra, marriage is possible within 23 to 25 years of age. If 7th lord or Venus is afflicted in birth chart or Navamsa chart, marriage may occur between 30 and 33 years of age.
8. During Dasa period of 7th lord, marriage may take place.
9. 7th lord from Venus or Moon may hasten marriage during their dasa and antra dasa.
10. Add degrees of planets indicated by constellations associated with Moon and 7th house lord. When Jupiter transits that rasi and amsa, marriage will take place.
11. Find out rasi and amsa by additions of degrees of Lagna lord, Venus and 7th lord. When Jupiter transits over that rasi and amsa, marriage is possible.

Married Life

A happy married life is a boon to the native in the present materialistic world. An unhappy married life has many reasons. Broadly speaking, adultery, widowhood, separation, divorce, harsh temperament of either partner, undutiful husband or wife. No issue, plural marriage, abnormal sexualities, dowry demands and ill-behaviour of in-laws etc. are the causes for an unhappy married life. These issues can be analysed astrologically through your horoscope.

Happy Married Life

In order to check and analyse the married life, the following yogas may be checked from the horoscope of husband and wife.

1. Jupiter and Venus being 7th lord and significator or 2nd and 11th houses.
2. If 7th house is occupied by its lord, receives aspect of a benefic planet and also 7th house lord from either Lagna or Moon is favourably disposed.

In the above two cases the married life is expected to be happy.

The natal houses of husband and wife are intersected, and have to be judged in conjunction with each other. From 1st and 7th houses of birth chart, you can judge the status, family, health, wealth, education etc. of husband. You can judge too the life of the husband and wife. If any of them is governed or aspected by an evil planet, the disparities and afflictions should follow. 1st and 7th houses favourably governed and aspected will result in a happy married life.

3. Moon receiving good aspects from Saturn, Venus and Jupiter is auspicious. The couple will give expression to their pleasant feelings and are playful during union.
4. Venus and Mars in good aspect are very advantageous provided they are not significators of 6th, 8th or 12th house.
5. If 7th house to Lagna or Moon sign is occupied by or aspected by benefics, by lordship, it will indicate a happy married life.
6. In a famale chart a good Jupiter in 7th will give a good husband and a happy married life.
7. If 7th or 8th house is occupied by a malefic but benefic in 9th house it indicates that the lady will enjoy a long lease of happy married life.
8. Jupiter lord of 2nd and 5th in 9th house in exaltation (Scorpio Lagna) and 9th lord exalted in Kendra (7th house) confer good fortune and good and happy married life.

9. If 7th house lord is exalted and Lagna lord occupies Lagna.
10. When 7th lord is a benefic planet and free from affliction, a happy married life is indicated.

Unhappy Married Life

A few yogas on this subject are detailed below:

1. A conjunction of Moon and Venus is not conducive to a happy married life.
2. If 7th lord is in 12th house or in 6th or 8th and malefic aspect or association.
3. If 7th house lord is afflicted, there may be quarrels and misunderstandings.
4. If Moon, Mars, Venus or the two luminaries (Sun and Moon) are in 7th house, the woman will be associated with another man at the instance of her husband, leading to an unhappy married life.
5. If there are malefics in 7th house and that planet is inimical to the 7th lord of ascendant, the marriage life will not be peaceful and happy.
6. If Mars and Venus are in any way afflicted.
7. 4th house denotes family members. When 4th house is afflicted it indicates disturbed family members.
8. When Rahu is in 4th house in a female's chart, an unhappy married life. If such Rahu is afflicted, she may have co-wives.
9. If 7th house is posited with malefic planet and 7th lord is his enemy, the woman will have constant quarrels with the husband.
10. When Saturn is in 7th house not being his own house or house of its exaltation, the woman will be disliked by her husband.
11. When Saturn, Rahu etc. transit in 7th house, Moon, Venus etc.. or aspect them, then during this transit, there will be misunderstandings, quarrels and unhappy incidents in the family.

Good and Honest Wife or Husband

In this materialistic world, it is rare to have a good and honest wife or husband. However, if one has, he or she must be congratulated. The following few yogas indicate such a wife or a husband. Normally the temperament of husband and wife must be judged from the characteristics of 7th lord and planets posited therein.

1. 7th lord when aspected or conjoined by favourable planets or well disposed or placed between benefics.
2. When 10th lord is powerful and favourably disposed and 7th lord is in favourable Navamsa.
3. When 7th lord is exalted, placed in its own sign or in friendly house and has good aspects and conjunction if any.
4. Venus, natural significator of 7th house if in favourable Navamsa and 10th lord is strong.
5. When 7th lord is strong, and aspected by Jupiter or conjoined with it, the wife or husband of the native is pious and religious.
6. If Moon is posited in favourable rasi, Navamsa etc., and is exalted or aspected by Jupiter, the wife will be faithful and moral.
7. Saturn as 7th lord, if strong, well disposed and is aspected by or conjoined with Jupiter or with any other planet, which is benefic, the native becomes respectful to Brahmins and Gods, and is religious.

Co-Wives or Plural Marriages

From 7th house of birth chart, the lords of 12th and 5th houses would be respectively the lords of 5th and 7th houses from 7th. Thus 12th house from the house of wife would receive three foreign influences of 6th and 7th houses alongwith foreign influence of Rahu. 6th house from Lagna being 12th from the house of wife denotes the pleasures of beds of wife. Foreign influences thereon would naturally make those pleasures foreign, which means that pleasures of beds of wife would be shared by other women or men, which tantamount to having many wives or co-wives at a time. Keeping this principle in view, we provide the following yogas:

1. If in a male chart the lords of 12th and 5th houses and Rahu have their influence on 6th house and its lord by association or aspect, and 7th lord is strongly placed in house of gain such as 11th house, one may have many women as wives at a time or a lady will have co-wives.
2. 4th place rules co-wives. When this house is afflicted and particularly conjoined or aspected by Rahu it indicates co-wives.
3. When Moon and Rahu join 4th house.
4. When malefics join Moon, Venus and Mercury.

5. If 7th lord and Venus are each posited in a dual rasi or amsa, the person will have a co-wife.
6. Moon or Venus in Gemini, Sagittarius and Pisces in 7th house or applying to several planets and unafflicted by the malefics indicate more than one wife.
7. Retrograde Jupiter in 7th with Mars and one of them in debilitation will indicate two marriages.
8. Two marriages can be predicted either through death or separation of first wife when:
    (i)   Venus, Saturn, Moon and Mars are in 7th house.
    (ii)   Venus in 4th or 8th posited in between Sun, Saturn and Mars.
    (iii) Pisces as Ascendant, 8th lord in Lagna associated or aspected by Rahu.
    (iv)   Saturn in 2nd, Rahu in 9th, 7th lord and a malefic in 3rd house.
    (v)   Cancer as Ascendant, Saturn in 8th, Mars in 4th, Saturn in 7th from Venus or Venus in 2nd.

Separation or Divorce

Various reasons of separation or divorce between husband and wife have been detailed already and now we have to deal with the subject astrologically.

In judging the horoscope the basic rule of "Separative Influence" is to be analysed which gives a clear view of its influences.

The rule says that, "Sun, Saturn, Rahu and 12th house lord and lords of sign occupied by these planets are Separative" in character, that is to say, these planets cause separation from or abandonment of the traits of the house etc., which they influence by association or aspect.

For example, if two or more of the above-mentioned planets influence the 4th house and its lord, one is forced to leave his home or country of birth. If they influence 7th house and its lord, one is separated from his wife or husband. If they influence 10th house and its lord and Sun, one has to be separated from the benefits of the ruling powers, viz. resigning from service, termination of service, change in profession, etc.

So in view of these, we provide a few yogas:

1. Jupiter in 7th house generally, even lord of 7th does bestow very unsatisfactory results. He causes great disappointments and dissatisfaction in married life. He causes undue delay in marriage.

2. Marital disorder may occur seeking separation when Venus is found in Kritika, Moola, Aridra or Jyeshtha nakshatras. Out of these Kritika is most inauspicious and gives very bad results.

3. When 7th lord is in 6th and afflicted by separative influence, there may be separation. Similarly, when 7th lord or significator joins the 6th lord and is afflicted by aspect or conjunction of malefics, similar results are likely. When strong Jupiter makes a link with the above combinations in any form, the separation may be saved but the husband and wife will experience quarrels.

4. 6th house denotes legal disputes and connection of malefic 6th lord with 7th house, 7th lord or significator may result in legal action and separation. Also when 7th lord or significator joins 6th house being afflicted by malefics.

5. When 7th house, 7th lord and significator all are afflicted, conjoined, associated or aspected by malefics, unhappiness in married life is indicated. Significator are Venus for males and Mars in case of females.

6. When Rahu and Saturn join Lagna, one is likely to face strife and separation in married life. When 7th lord is retrograde and is also afflicted, similar results are experienced.

7. When in a female chart, Aries or Scorpio Lagna rise and 7th lord is weak, combust, retrograde and is also afflicted, she will be abandoned by her husband.

8. If combination of Sun and Mars in either horoscope is in 2nd, 7th or 8th house, it holds out excellent prospects for discarding, separation and disunion. It does not necessarily involve loss of partner.

9. To analyse marriage, affliction to Venus by situation, association or aspects of malefics have an adverse effect on morals. Venus represents the other partner of marriage.

10. When lords of 2nd and 7th houses are in constellation of evil lords, particularly in the constellation of 6th lord and are afflicted, there will be separation, divorce, litigation etc. between the couple.

Planets in 7th House

General Tips

Having discussed various aspects of marriage in detail, we now provide our readers general tips to check the married life.

A planet in a house of sign other than his own is like a man in another man's house, where he has limited freedom of action. While he can normally express his views and nature he is fundamentally subject to the rules of his host.

A planet in 7th house is a significator of marriage and marriage partner and indicates more immediate, obvious and superficial results.

The sign in which planet is posited is of great importance. For example, Jupiter in Capricorn in 7th is debilitated. If well aspected give favourable marriage conditions but with reservations. But if Saturn, 7th house lord otherwise called dispositor, is afflicted, the marriage conditions will generally gradually deteriorate and the marriage will have Saturnian effects. So the effects are to be judged.

The following is the results of each planet in 7th house to be modified on the basis of the above rules and lines. It applies to both sexes.

1. *SUN*: It is not a happy and desirable position. The partner will be of an independent view, proud, ambitious, generous, honourable and of loyal nature only if Sun is not afflicted. If afflicted he or she will be arrogant, dominating, selfish and extravagant. Marriage to a person of high or good social status is indicated. Business or social advancement may come through marriage.

Sun in 7th usually delays marriage towards the middle life. In case of affliction of Sun, the partner can be a social climber, vain, boastful and of ostentatious character and extravagant. The best way to deal with such a situation is to submit to the other partner, and avoid domestic quarrels. The affliction to Sun also indicates formidable opposition to the marriage from parents with financial authority and ambitions which may cause wrecking of career or the woman may be abandoned by her husband causing unhappiness, separation and divorce. She may suffer from diseases, irreligious and delayed marriage. Such a woman will hate sex acts, which may also become a cause for separation. Aspect of Jupiter on Sun will reduce the evil effects to some extent.

2. *MOON*: Moon in 7th house is not generally favourable, for it imparts a too strong tendency towards fluctuation and change in married life. However, it indicates a romantic marriage, a husband of very susceptible nature, whose affection may stray. If well aspected, indicates an exacting partner. When afflicted, indicates nagging and constant harping on peace in married life. The lady becomes fastidious and capricious, very undecided in choice of marriage partner. Without strong aspects, Moon indicates marriage at the age of about 24 to 28 years.

Malefic aspects to Moon without any benefic aspect by Jupiter or Venus cause death of partner, separation or divorce. This may not prevent a second marriage.

Ladies with 7th house Moon are moody, love their husbands, are fond of opposite sex, tender-hearted and jealous. Love dominates them. Aspect of Venus to Moon often results in love marriage, unconventional rebel marriages but aspect of Jupiter gives an arranged marriage.

Moon in 7th house being in Taurus, Cancer or Pisces blesses the woman with a good and happy married life. Moon in Capricorn, Aries, Scorpio or Aquarius is bad for a happy married life.

3. *MARS*: Mars in 7th nouse causes *kujadosha* or Mangleek subject to exceptions. It is always a dangerous position even when well aspected. It is of two extremes, positive and individualistic nature even for a partnership.

Position indicates widowhood in youth. Such ladies are sex-ridden, and will have extra-marital relations. Benefic aspect of Venus or Jupiter will ward off above bad results. Frequent quarrels in married life often leading to misunderstanding and separation.

In ladies chart, forceful and energetic, also ambitious, masterful, self-assertive, capable, rash in temperament and an industrious partner. If afflicted, one will be irascible, aggressive, quarrelsome, destructive, vicious, violent, brutal and murderous. The worst affliction to Mars is from Saturn.

Affliction from Jupiter or 8th house lord will bring friction over the partner's extravagance, while bad aspects to Venus will have additional effects of adultery.

If Mars is afflicted in Cancer, Scorpio or Pisces in 7th house, partner may be a drunkard. If afflicted by Saturn when Mars is in earthy sign indicates delay in marriage, great difficulty in finding a match, lustfulness and if marriage takes place, it will be hasty.

Generally Mars in 7th house denotes passionate nature, antagonism or opposition and of questionable character. It also causes quarrels, leads to violence, separation and divorce. A headstrong and independent partner. As indicated earlier, also causes death of husband through fever or operation. When Mars is in fixed sign, through an accident, if in Cardinal sign, the end is sudden in all cases.

After marriage life course will change and create difficulties, upset existing conditions.

4. *MERCURY*: A strong benefic and well aspected Mercury in 7th house indicates a lucky marriage, a considerate and rich husband, but he will lack in sex, causing bickerings on this account.

The partner will be bright, changeable, shrewd, critical, and clever but somewhat unreliable. Native may flirt.

An afflicted Mercury indicates bickerings, mental or physical cruelty, quarrels or nagging. May also indicate afflicted health, stupid partner, partner may be impatient, mentally or physically afflicted.

Affliction by Saturn or Mars indicates sex perversion like sadism or masochism.

Marriage is influenced by relations and may come through travel, correspondence or advertisement. Partner will be younger than native. Any affliction to Mercury indicates worry through marriage, legal actions and difficulty in choosing partner.

5. *JUPITER*: Jupiter in 7th house in Capricorn or Aquarius causes separation, bickerings and even divorce. In mutable signs causes more than one marriage, though affliction produces irregular unions. Wedding date in this case sometimes is postponed also when afflicted by Saturn or Mercury.

Jupiter in Cancer, Taurus or Libra indicates conjugal happiness provided it is not afflicted.

Partner will be generous, optimistic, good natured, healthy, prosperous if not rich and conventional. A good Jupiter in 7th house indicates prosperity through marriage but not a happy union. Afflicted Jupiter indicates a boastful, bombastic and self-indulgent partner.

The position of Jupiter in 7th house when not strong by sign, aspect etc. denotes marriage to widower, or to a middle-aged person for money and social advancement.

When Jupiter is aspected by Mars, the couple will enjoy sex life to the maximum and be extravagant. When afflicted by Mercury, he will be vain, conceited, hypocritical and possibly dishonest. If by Sun, vain and overbearing. By Moon or Venus, prodigal, of wandering nature and affectionate and extravagant. By Saturn it causes separation through divorce or death of husband. A good Jupiter in 7th house is an asset. But badly afflicted will bring bad luck and even serious misfortune. In such a case the husband is noble but will fail to understand his wife. One gets married between 22 and 25 years of age.

6. *VENUS:* Venus in 7th house has no guarantee for a successful and happy marriage but indicates a good deal of affection. Much depends on aspects. Aspect of Mars or Saturn makes one immoral. Connections of Venus with 12th house lord in any way denote immense pleasures of beds with opposite sex. Jupiter's aspects give soothing effects. An unaspected Venus, on the other hand, may considerably restrict the mutual affection, or at least prevent its proper expression.

Venus in 7th of a lady's chart indicates that she is sexy, fond of the opposite sex, expert in sex enjoyment. She always longs for love, marries for love but fails. The husband will be kind, gentle and affectionate. But when afflicted will be vain, hazy, self-indulgent, spends much money and time on women.

It is best when Venus is in Taurus, Cancer or Pisces in 7th house. Not favourable in Scorpio causing early death of partner. Saturn in 4th or 5th indicates domestic coldness and isolation. Leo is most favourable but in this case, interest in marriage is often apparently only to have children. The husband is more or less is of a secondary consideration.

Venus in 7th house delays marriage quite apart from any affliction that may be present. In Libra sign, shows little interest in opposite sex and no particular desire for marriage but for companionship and for a life of ease and luxury, viz. one is fond of amusements, but in a suitable environment, plenty of friends and sufficient money.

Affliction from Mars brings impetuous and extravagant love affairs. Any type of affliction in any house to Venus by Saturn is the strongest possible influence preventing marriage.

7. *SATURN*: Again a dangerous and dreaded position like Mars, as it indicates separation, restrictions, avoids close associations with others. If Saturn is aspected by malefics, one will not be married or it causes delay in marriage and often partner is much older. Such persons are pessimistic, of dogmatic views and hardly adjustable to change in their life. If aspected by Mars, sex life will indicate malefic results and partner will be much below the status of the native. If Mercury and Saturn are in 7th house, the husband will be impotent.

Saturn in 7th house causes hindrances and misconceptions, not only in marriage but in all relations with other people. Usually elements of disappointment are indicated. An afflicted Saturn indicates that marriage will be a sorrowful and tragic experience. Partner will be cold, · avaracious, resentful, mean, selfish, cruel or may become a chronic. ¹ When afflictions are more violent, death of partner will be through accident, operation or by separation.

8. *RAHU*: Delayed marriage may cause separation or an early widowhood. Such persons or ladies are moody and difficult for friendship, being too greedy and selfish. May marry out of caste or some may get into a scandalous position. Moon conjoining Rahu causes hysteria to lady. Aspect of Saturn or Mars indicates marriage with low caste. Unconventional marriage, may bring dishonour to family and engender misery. Rahu in Aries or Scorpio indicates widowhood.

9. *KETU* : Such persons or ladies are of loose morals, quarrelsome, and treacherous. Connections with the opposite sex, unhappy married life. Unconventional marriage between 20 and 24 years of age. When Saturn or Mars aspects Ketu, partner will allow the other partner to go with the opposite sex for selfish gain or one will keep prostitutes or a brothel. Aspects of Jupiter to Ketu in Sagittarius or Pisces shows mitigation of the above effects.

Other Positions

1.   If 7th house is posited with mixed set of planets, both benefic and malefic, married life will be average, but if afflicted, remarriage.

2. If in 7th house there is a weak planet, aspected by benefics, the woman may be put away by her husband or vice versa.
3. If Moon, Mars and Venus or Sun and Moon occupy 7th house the native may associate with the opposite sex.
4. If 7th house is owned or aspected by malefic, she may be childless, so says Jatak Tatva. But in author's views, 5th and 9th houses should also be checked alongwith the chart of her husband.
5. If 7th house and Lagna occupied by malefics, the woman will become widow after years of marriage unless there are good aspects of Jupiter, etc.

Lord of 7th in Houses

So far we have studied various aspects of marriage and married life, but the students become confused, when they find that 7th house lord is posited in another house, so, for their guidance, we now explain the effects of 7th house lord in different houses of horoscope. When 7th lord is in these houses, the effects as shown below can be modified according to sign of house and aspects on the house.

1st House: It is Lagna. When 7th lord is in Lagna it indicates good marriage and she will love her husband, although she will choose her husband and have an arranged marriage; the husband need not be a relation.

In case of males, one will have intrigues with other women also of sharp intellect, loose morals; is prudent, skilful, and may suffer from rheumatism or gout particularly if Lagna rises in Scorpio and 7th lord is in Lagna. If Mars or Rahu are in 7th house, and Venus in Scorpio, the native may be a debauch. Similar results can be expected if Lagna rises as Libra and Venus, Saturn, Mars and Rahu are in 7th house.

2nd House: Unconventional marriage or love marriage, maybe to a relation. A happy married life but financial difficulties will be in life.

In male horoscope, one will be a henpecked husband. Results will be happy in case of Aries and Scorpio Lagna. In other Lagnas finances will be average. If for Aries Lagna, Venus is in conjunction with Jupiter and Mars in 2nd house, native will be very rich.

3rd House: Marriage to close relations or close family friends. Late marriage after 25th year and preferably in 27th year, which will be happy. If Mars or Saturn aspects, relations will blame the girl for marriage.

In male's chart if 7th lord here is combust, the wife of the native will either be shortlived or sickly. If 5th house lord and house are strong and well disposed favourable results for children.

4th House: An unhappy conjugal life. The native will be truthful and virtuous. If aspected by Mars, Saturn or Rahu, the marriage will be with a low caste man and unhappy.

In male chart, one will do well in business if 7th lord is not afflicted but aspected by favourable planet.

5th House: Marriage through profession with a selfmade man. A happy married life. Marriage will be approved by parents.

In male's chart, native will be meritorious, wealthy and happy. The results will be favourable in case of Gemini Lagna when 7th Lord Jupiter in conjunction with Venus is in 5th. Also in case of Scorpio Lagna when 7th lord Venus and Jupiter are in 5th place from Lagna.

6th House: Love or self-arranged marriage opposed by relatives, the native will love her husband, the marriage will be unhappy.

In male's chart, his wife will be sick, he himself will become peevish, irritable and unhappy. Unless benefics aspect on 7th house or its lord, his business or profession may be unsuccessful.

7th House: Generally this denotes love marriage. If aspected by Mercury or Jupiter, the marriage will be approved by parents, otherwise arranged marriage in early age. A happy married life.

In male's chart, the native enjoys a happy married life, his wife will be faithful and pious. If 7th lord is with Rahu, Saturn or Mars, his wife will be uncontrollable, haughty and unchaste. She may be involved in an accident.

8th House: A most dreadful position. Late or delayed marriage. Marriage will be self-arranged, out of act of folly or foolish passions which may result in happiness. If malefics occupy 8th, she will become a widow.

In male's chart, above results will be good. Gain from marriage The native may suffer from disease of intestine or abdomen.

9th House: Gain through marriage amongst relations and known family and generally happy marriage unless afflicted by malefics.

In male's chart native may be benefited by his wife or in-laws shall be lucky.

10th House: A happy marriage chosen by the girl from amongst the colleagues and co-workers.

In male's chart, native will be truthful, pious and happy. If Lagna, rises in Gemini, Sagittarius or Pisces and 7th lord is in 10th, native will be highly educated, will build his own career by his merits and efforts and will get power, authority and fame. In case of Aries Lagna, results will not be so favourable if 9th lord is not favourably disposed.

11th House: It is a house of gain. So a good and gainful marriage arranged by the parents and amongst the family members.

In male's chart, unless 5th lord and house are strong, the marriage will be unhappy, his children may be short-lived.

12th House: Unconventional and self-arranged marriage. If Jupiter is in 12th house, the marriage will be approved by parents and will be of average nature. A few people say unhappy marriage, but in author's views aspects should be considered.

In male's chart, loss of domestic peace. If 4th lord and house are favourable, family peace may be restored occasionally, bad health of wife, and short journeys etc, are indicated.

In a Nutshell

We have discussed in detail, the possibility and effects of married life in male and female charts astrologically. You can check your charts from these ready reckoners or contact the author for consultations and guidance.

HUSBANDS

The husband and wife or partner, if married legally or by an agreement, are the wheels of a chariot to make life happy and successful. If both understand each other and supplement their efficiencies, deficiencies properly and knowingly, there is full scope to avert frustration and disappointment.

The characteristics of the sign rising on Ascendant should correspond to oneself whereas the rising on Descendant should be considered as that of the partner, viz. Aries-Libra, Taurus-Scorpio etc.

The following description of each sign will be helpful to understand each other and to adjust one's physical as well as psychological behaviour and temperaments.

1. Aries

The husband will be a very desirable person, usually he selects a beautiful, clever and good wife. Generous and beautiful, romantic but a spendthrift. Rash and passionate. He is an electrically charged dynamo. One can depend on him for excitement. But in terms of security and contentment, of soothing love, the wife is in wrong hands. Beware of it.

He has creative energy, is passionate and warm, impatient, bold and confident. Generous and intolerant. Unless his wife is a Scorpio, he is passionate with every and any woman who could ask. Idealistic and susceptible to sentiments. When he is in love he is then scrupulously faithful, loyal and devoted. She should be ready to greet him with all her charms as and when he is with her or comes back from his job. In case she neglects his romance, she can be heartbroken.

He is possessive and jealous to the extreme. Due to his rash behaviour and driving, he can get head or face injury, cuts or burns. He may change jobs frequently unless he becomes his own boss. Devoted to children.

Professions

Professions connected with him are army, defence department, surgeons, police, chemists, law, iron, steel, machines, factories, industry or sports goods.

What Girls Should Do

He wants a fair lady, ultra feminine. He expects praise from her but never a slave. When his ego has been wounded and things beyond his control happen it will make him sarcastic, bitter and cruel, so she should understand him. He believes in forgive and forget. She will have to like all his friends. He will dominate the home or leave it, she has to adjust. He is a man's man. Devoted to children and a little bossy over them, but not to worry at all. He cannot submit. Without losing her individuality, she should try not to destroy his masculinity. He does not like her to run to clubs every night.

So the lady, has to manage all this to be a good housewife and have a hold over him, so she can enjoy a happy married life.

Taurus

A husband born in Taurus Lagna, is devoted to his wife, reliable, generous and faithful. He will never neglect the house and her needs. He likes to see his wife well dressed, attractive and pleasing. Cooperative and will love her extensively. Practical, not very romantic, lacks in taking decision. She should not shout at him. He is of stubborn mood, he will protect her always. She should apologise to him for her mistake. He is extremely patient, too practical, likes his freedom too much. He will not like or tolerate her bullying him in public.

Financially, he is usually excellent. Less accumulation of wealth. He does not like her to be a kitchen slave. Affectionate, loving, warm and a sympathetic father.

He loves comforts, beautiful surroundings and a pleasing partner. Sexual attachment is a prominent attribute and even temporary separation is felt by them to be unbearable. Persons born with Kritika and Mrigasira are bit rash in their manifestation but with Rohini are fond of easy living and luxurious. His love is plain, simple and honest.

It is true he is not very romantic but is strongly attracted to the opposite sex but not aggressively, does not waste time chasing anybody. He seldom worries and not nervous. Love of food and drink makes him overweight which should be avoided. He starts with solid foundation and progresses slowly, until he builds a stable business and settles down in service and has a stable bank balance through hard labour. He is impressed by bigness. His ideas are sensible.

Professions

He can be an accountant, a double career will be his speciality. He may trade in cosmetics, luxury goods, scents, jewels etc. Any business connected with finance, agriculture or music. Transport business, cinema actors, film producers etc. Dealers in ladies' garments, school dresses etc.

3. Gemini

A Gemini husband wants a *Yes wife*. He can put an abrupt end to romance or married life if he finds it a source of expense and loss and cannot tolerate an overbearing wife. He has changeable personality. Love, ecstasy, intelligence, idealism, sorrow or joy—these merciful changes of Gemini's expression are very fascinating. He can change love affairs, his job, his residence as quickly as he can change his mind.

He will be slender, agile, taller than average; many have sharp features. The eyes are restless, alert and quick moving. He is sympathetic, friendless and unusually quick, but has graceful movements. Practical and adjustable. Argumentative, witty, sharply satirical and of changeable nature.

In love, he gives a nice sense of warm security. He has a restless and unpredictable spirit. He likes people, is a favourite with the opposite sex, and has exquisite taste. After meeting him, you will find him exciting, interesting, intelligent and feel drawn towards him. He is not possessive or suspicious. Love is not a strictly physical relationship with this man. He may refrain from being demonstrative to children outwardly.

What Girls should do

Keep things cool and light, and not be very possionate or dramatic. Do not bore him always. Be as alert and interested in life as he is. He seeks a mental companion above all else. A Geminian tries to discard old friends for new ones due to his nature. There is seldom very deep lasting attachment to old memories, places, people and things. He is gregarious and hates, even fears, being alone for long periods. So do not leave him alone.

Professions

Geminians have interest in varied jobs as they are active, alert, and industrious. Being good speakers, intelligent and humorous, are fit for politics. Other professions are brokers, share market agents, businessmen, secretaries, scientists and advocates. Also journalists, travelling agents and jobs connected with them.

Cancer

Cancer-born husbands are devoted to their wives. They would like to marry a homely girl and not a career one. They keep them cheerful, pleasing them in all ways. If critical, he interferes in routine household matters and creates unpleasant atmosphere.

Of changeable mood, has uncanny sense of publicity, has ups and downs in life. Of fertile imagination, sentimental, sympathetic and talkative. Emotional and has a strong conventional nature and is romantic. Life without romance is monotonous to him, loyal, sincere and affectionate in love but lacks in expression. He is secretive, generous and helpful to needy persons.

Being moody and considerate, he flirts and is fickle. His changing personality puzzles you. Devoted and emotional. In case the birth is in Pushya Nakshatra, forced separation due to calamity or inevitable divorce. In case of Ashlesha he is skilful in handling the partner and establishing himself independently from the family to create an empire of his own. Selection of girls for love or marriage is a problem for him.

What Girls should do

An easy way to hold him is to work on his emotions. Be dressed nicely. Speak sweet words, respect his mother and do not throw away his old things. Go with him to pleasure resorts, clubs etc. He is fond of good food, money and children.

Professions

Cancerians have commercial career. May be sailor in Navy, Shipping Department, import or export, transport and travel. Also a good caterer, restaurant manager, orator, preacher, contractor. Interested in developing vedic and sacred texts.

5. Leo

Leonians, despite their generosity and royal nature, are deprived of a real and enjoyable married life for one reason or another in later life. Being fiery they have intense love and sincerity towards their partner but they rarely get a sportive and jolly partner. They are influenced by the opposite sex. Persons with Poorva Phalguni Nakshatra enjoy married life in the real sense whereas with Uttra Phalguni it is not so. They are dominating and imposing.

Leo husbands are exciting and attractive to other ladies. If his wife understands him and agrees with him, then she will be liked, admired and loved. He cannot tolerate ill repute. Passionate, of loving nature, rash in temperament, ambitious, generous, warm-hearted and magnanimous. Very independent views, practical nature, constructive, active, bold and a true friend. A Leo is sexy, and will not accept superficial love. He wants to live in style and wants you to live elegantly.

Intellectual, of majestic appearance, commanding and dignified. It is hard to stand in front of Lion-Leo. Do not find faults with him. By nature, he is totally loyal and sincere. If love is missing from his life, he will simply pine away. You must walk with him in dignity and with majestic appearance when he takes you to clubs, restaurants etc. He is jealous in romance, he cannot tolerate sharing your bed with your husband if he is your paramour or friend. Suspicious, he cannot tolerate your absence from home. To call him a flirt is your biggest folly. So he must get respect and confidence from you, otherwise you may lose him.

What Girls should do

It is my advice to you ladies, that once you just win his heart with sincerity, not with selfish motive, then enjoy with him, he is so ardent that he will leave everybody, even his family members for you, forgo comforts for your security. This is his secret of life. If your relations are deep and sincere then he will protect you. Loyal and sincere, he is a superb organiser, whatever he says, he means it. Forgiveness and sympathy are his basic traits. Extravagant, gastric, ulcer, accidents to arms, ankle or legs but will recoup early. He wants first class luxuries all through life and spends freely on fun and pleasures. He is generous with loans to the friends. In case of an emergency, he never shirks his duty.

Profession

Leos can be best educators, politicians, occupy high positions in Government; of executive ability, managers of big concerns, corporation, director, captain, sales manager, etc.

6. Virgo

A Virgo-born husband is practical and adjustable. He provides all comforts to his wife and children. Change is his basic nature— wandering, change of residence and environments, etc. Believes in show business. Fond of learning, active mind, good mental and intellectual abilities, critical, emotional, lacks in decision making and self-confidence. Industrious and ambitious of wealth. Expert in finding faults with others. Careful and sensitive. Methodical, will face ups and downs in life. Limited progeny. He builds castles in the air, not practical but lethargic. Elusive in love. He is of wiry build, has clarity in his expressions and features are attractive , has grace and charm. Calm and soothing. He is unquestionably dependable and sincere. In romance he is called *Cold Fish*. Incapable of sitting very long. He is lavish not in love but in spending money. Saves for old age. Selfish. He likes truth, punctuality, prudence and discretion.

What Girls should do

In case you love him, do not pin your hopes on him; if your heart is hungry for love, you will starve. He seeks quality not quantity, He considers it a waste to spend money in clubs, restaurants, so avoid it. A difficult man to stir emotionally. Once his love flame is ignited and he is deeply in love with you then he will never fluctuate.

Professions

Virgos are slaves to work, hard taskmasters and like to be left alone. So fit for becoming a broker, accountant, lawyer, journalist, engineer, surgeon and connected with liquids, etc.

7. Libra

A Libra husband is cheerful, passionate, of adjustable nature, accommodative and will provide for his wife and family all comforts of life. Good demonstrator of love. In case he does not get a response from you, he will become disappointed but will not seek divorce. Fond of dress, beauty, perfumes, art and music. Of fertile imagination. Affectionate, sexy, passionate, kind and generous. Fond of the opposite sex, he has a strong conjugal affection and for him the most important thing is pleasure. Your connection with him will be too strong to break. Love and Libra are synonymous. He will not ever lose interest in the opposite sex. He cannot say 'No' to anybody. Once you catch him passionately, he will be a miserable prisoner of love. He is terribly trustworthy. He is on the whole a balanced, harmonious man. He hates quarrels, is amiable, not dishonest. Cultural shows and parties are his favourite places, where he can enjoy good food, wine and mingle with the opposite sex. Normally has sound finances.

What Girls should do

Keep the house in order. He needs harmony for a stable home, so please adjust. Do not shout at him, he does not like you to excel him in anything.

Professions

A Government servant or officer. Will lead a public social life. Best suited for law, chemist, liquid items, electrical engineer, transport, Navy or painters etc. Dealing with articles of feminine interest and luxury or amusement items. Also can be writer, musician, singer and actor.

8. Scorpio

A Scorpion husband has a good personality, well proportioned body, sharp and clearly drawn features. He will care for his wife and honour her. Rash in temperament, of adjustable nature and has a controlled nature. He is quick, frank, critical, and has keen judgement. A few are of practical nature. Impulsive, forceful, has constructive and destructive tendencies. Emotional, cunning but very true, loyal, faithful and reliable. Also revengeful, restless and selfish.

A Scorpio husband is intense, dynamic, energetic in romance and love but of complex moods. Highly passionate and sexy. He cannot tolerate any criticism. In finance he is lucky. Extravagant and cannot remain idle. He fights boldly odds of life and never surrenders. Fond of contests and travels. He is invincible in love, has twin traits of passions and reasons. Enjoys good health and luxury. Determined and likes to be respected. He can be saint or sinner. Law abiding to the last moment until somebody provokes him to violence. Choosy about friends and wife. A stern father, a good advisor and friend to children.

What Girls should do

You should be of adjustable nature, knowing how to please and contain him, otherwise you will lose him. You should not be sarcastic to, and critical of him, he will not be able to bear it. Be patient. Do not drink and be avenging. Do not allow him to be a bad Scorpio, otherwise he will create anarchy, lawlessness, and destruction as he is a firebrand and dangerous.

Professions

Scorpions dial with chemistry, medicine, insurance, maternity department and surgeons. Research work, C.I.D. detectives, iron and steel work, military and naval department. Can be good politicians, orators and composers of great musical works, actors and dramatists.

9. Sagittarius

A Sagittarius husband has a well-developed body. Tall, slender, generally long or oval face, charming appearance, graceful look and handsome. Normally restless, flares up quickly for a short time. Fond of games, sports and clubs which are more important to him than his family life. A person of morality and dignity. Active, impulsive, fond of travelling and outdoor life. Optimistic, frank, seeks casual relations, likes variety not only in sex. The married life is generally happy and prosperous.

What Girls should do

If you are his friend, wife or mistress, do not be jealous, or be suspicious, weep, nag or threaten to leave him. But allow him freedom. Just do what he wants. In travelling accompany him. Do not restrict him. Fond of overeating good food, so please him. Be not of vindictive nature.

Professions

He can be a good teacher, orator, bank employee or politician. Attached to religious and educational institutions. Editing and publishing will be rewarding. He can be a master of company law, civil engineer, contractor, on foreign assignments. Speculation will not be helpful.

10. Capricorn

A Capricorn husband is not emotional and romantic but is economical, self-willed, reserved, pensive, reasonable, thoughtful and of practical nature. Calculative and business like, will have push and confidence. Desirous of power and authority, ability for managing and organising. Melancholy and seriousness surround him. A stern discipline and self-denial is the nature. Never deviates an inch from his decision.

In romance, not emotional, cautious approach to opposite sex, not bold and rash and never takes the lead, the opposite sex remains worried and puzzled by his hesitancy and undemonstrative love. More contended. Interferes with other people's affairs. Marries for money or social status. He becomes nervous in the presence of the opposite sex. Normally his married life is solid, he abhors divorce, but when he does it is final. So be careful. He is interested in planned physical side of love. He is not a fiery lover but deliciously romantic.

What Girls should do

Be moderate and do not hate his relatives, parents, brothers and friends. Insulting, hurting and making false statements should be avoided. Do not be of a vindictive mind. Do not interfere in his affairs. Do not suggest unless asked for. Be of adjustable nature and helpful to him. If he is wrong, be polite with him.

Professions

Contractor, cement broker, dealer in scientific instruments. Physician, gain through lands, mines, kerosene or petrol, chemicals etc.

11. Aquarius

He is generally kind and tranquil by nature. Law abiding. Soft spoken and courteous, uses frequently the word "Friend". Handsome appearance, will become flabby in middle age. Often has feminine characteristics. Intelligent and researching mind. They spend little time with the family and children but sympathetic, accommodative and generous, care for the children, educate them and encourage them.

Actually they are funny, perverse, original, conceited and independent but are also diplomatic and timid. Not many friends. He can read others' characters and likes solitude which should not be interrupted. Strong in likes and dislikes. Likes team work. Both fortunate and unfortunate. In love and romance, he does not show his love, but is cold, so if you are passionate, will not be satisfied. Chooses intelligent and beautiful girls. When heartbroken, leaves without fuss. He may not be a good breadwinner as he is not greedy. Hard worker.

What Girls should do

He is unconventional, so bear with it. Do not interrupt his solitude. Give him a chance to express freely and frankly. Do not try to dictate to him. Due to his rigid moral codes and high ideals yours cooperation will make him successful in life. He has love for cleanliness, so follow it.

Professions

Politics fascinates him. Sports absorbs him. Automobile, medical discoveries, authors, astronauts, alcoholics, pianists interest him.

12. Pisces

To recognise a Pisces husband, look for elastic and mobile features, more dimples than wrinkles. Skin is silky and soft. Big and protruding eyes, tall, face fleshy. Quick in understanding, inspirational, easygoing, loving, truthful, has little worldly ambitions, not so fond of ranks, power or leadership. Wealth holds little attractions for him. Lack of intensity, careless. One is only impressed by charming manners and his lazy good nature. Very little will goad him to violent actions. Passionate, affectionate and charitable. Philosophical and leads a romantic life. At times, can be sarcastic.

Attracted to romantic life, prefers beauty and intellect of the partner. Suspicious nature kills his love but he likes flattery. Will lead a happy married life. Faith in him and he will never betray you. Speaks slowly, thinks gently and minds his own business. He can be easily hurt but cannot be fooled. Tempted to fancies of life. Sometimes he is outspoken. Although he shirks from competitions, he even reaches heights. Frank and generous. Humorous, master of satire. Helpful to others. He hates to answer direct questions.

What Girls should do

When your husband is Pisces-born, do not ask him direct questions, he will be offended. Be happy with him. His friends should be entertained well. Avoid suspecting him. Cultivate push, be generous but not over liberal. Do not allow him to live on others' hopes and promises.

Professions

He can be successful as accountant, banker, music and opera house, cinema, occult science, actors and a good businessman also and can be a good liaison officer, managing director, organisor, Navy or Shipping Corporations. Dealing in drinks, beverages, cosmetics, chemicals, medical and education departments.

LOVE MARRIAGE

Love marriage is an arranged marriage by the boy and girl through their own choice denouncing the customs. There is first the moment of attraction, sometimes it is spontaneous and sometimes the relations grow slowly and result in love.

Astrologically, the mutual harmony between the couples or lovers which determines mutual attraction, harmony and adaptability between two persons of opposite sex can be analysed to find out whether such conditions exist in the horoscope of both or they are of lasting nature or break. The first part is checked from the horoscope and the second part from the directions.

5th house of birth charts indicates customs and traditions. Similarly religion and religious customs are studied from 9th house. 7th house stands for partner and marriage. Love marriage means abandoning customs and traditions. So in such charts 5th house is occupied by strong planets or by own lord or emotional planets. The strongest planet for creating an urge for love marriage or relations is Saturn followed by Rahu. In a male's chart if Venus is affected or afflicted through conjunction or aspect by Saturn or Rahu a love marriage is indicated.

So 5th, 7th and 9th houses and their lords are involved in love marriage. Both the lords are shown in conjunction or in trine or sextile, in 5th, 7th or 9th, 10th or 11th. In certain cases 9th lord joins lords of 5th or 7th. In short, formula for love marriage will be as follows.

1. Lord of 5th + Lord of 7th
2. Lord of 7th + Lord of 9th
3. Lord of 5th + Lord of 9th

The aspects between the lords of above houses should be angular.

In a female's chart Mars plays the part of Venus in a male's horoscope. So if Mars is aspected or conjoined in her chart with Rahu or Saturn or aspects are there, she flirts with a male and has illicit relations. Marriage depends on the disposition of Venus, Rahu, Saturn and Moon in the male birth chart.

It is needless to say that the conjunction of above planets must be either in 5th, 7th (primarily), 10th, 11th or 1st houses (secondary). Otherwise the prospective couples may have an opportunity to come together for a long time without any prospects of successful marriage.

If the above conjunction falls in 6th, 8th, or 12th houses, frustration due to one reason or another cannot be ruled out. Willingly or unwillingly the lovers have to sacrifice their love life and have to join their hands with some unexpected and unknown partners in marriage.

Love at First Sight

As a matter of fact, this type of marriage cannot be brought into the above category. It mainly emerges out of conjunction or aspect of Mars-Venus. It prompts the individuals to conceal or declare their love. It is doubtful if all the cases blossom into the sweet wedding as the tide of passions lasts for a short time.

Successful Love Marriage

A love marriage can be successful if the following configurations are available in the charts of both sexes.

1. If radical Mars of a female horoscope is aspected by radical Rahu or Saturn of a male chart.
2. If Venus of male and Mars of female chart are conjoined, aspected or in mutual kendras or trikona.
3. When Venus in male and Mars in female horoscopes are afflicted by Saturn and Rahu at birth and male's Saturn aspects female's Venus. Rahu also in similar conditions, results in similar effects.
4. When Venus in male chart is in 12th house and Mars in same house in female chart they are responsible for many romances.
5. When 5th house is occupied or aspected by a strong planet out of Mars, Moon and Venus, a person is very emotional and liable to fall in love with the opposite sex very easily.
6. If there is a malefic planet in 9th house, one is sure to go for a love marriage, as one will not honour customs etc.
7. For successful love marriage, a study of relative and mutual disposition of Mars, Venus and Rahu is essential as they cause sex perversion. Study of Saturn, a primary cause of misery is to be made.
8. If Mars and Venus have exchanged their places in the charts of the couple, the love marriage will be a great success.
9. If Mars of female falls in Rahu's position in male chart, the marriage will end in a divorce due to sex perversion from female or if Venus of male is in Rahu of female, the separation or divorce will be due to sex perversion of male. Similarly

Rahu in female chart should not have any bad aspect on Venus in male chart as it would aggravate the sex perversion.

10. In the same manner Saturn will cause misery due to poverty, disease etc. after marriage.

11. The comparison of Sun, Mars, Moon and Venus in both horoscopes is a matter of vital importance and can be checked as below:

   (i)   If Sun in one chart has the same longitude as Moon or rising sign in the other horoscope, it is conducive to good marriage.

   (ii)   If Sun in male and Moon in female's chart have same longitude, mutual attraction and congeniality are the result.

   (iii)   If Sun in female and Mars in male charts have same longitude, there will be attraction between the two.

   (iv)   If Moon in one and Ascendant or Sun in the other chart have same longitude it is conducive to harmony.

   (v)   Sun in one in good aspect to Ascendant or Moon in the other, as above.

   (vi)   Moon in one, in conjunction or good aspect with Lagna or Sun in the other, exercises good influence.

   (vii)   Sun in one to Sun in the other in good aspect is good.

   (viii)   Moon in one to Moon in the other in good aspect or in conjunction leads to good relations.

   (ix)   Sun and Venus having same longitude in each other's charts show much pleasure and enjoyment. Moon and Venus have the same effects.

   (x)   Mars and Venus of same longitude in each other's charts leads to mutual attraction, though it may not be endurable.

12. Jupiter and Saturn of the same longitude, Jupiter and Venus and Mars and Saturn of the same longitude in each chart indicates mutual love and harmony except the last one which indicates quarrels etc.

5

LOVE, NATURE AND SEX

Love means warm affection, benevolence, sexual passions. It also includes mutual attraction.

We have already explained love at first sight and love marriage in the previous chapter.

Now we shall explain love nature of an individual and the love sign which is amiable to him/her in life.

MOON

Moon affects the human life the most. It indicates Mind. It is the most important planet in Hindu Astrology, all yogas are counted from Moon, matching of horoscopes is made from Moon, etc. The sign in which Moon is placed in your birth chart is called your *Janam Rasi* and is vital for all predictions and readings throughout life.

In females Moon too plays an important role. The monthly menstruation of a woman is due to interaction of Moon and Mars.

Moon denotes mind, intellect, emotions, temperament, sex attitude, woman's generative organs. Also signifies mother, charming eyes, breasts, love for pleasure and beauty, family life, personal and private affairs. Also Moon rules over our working of mind, likes and dislikes.

So in Hindu astrology Moon has a significant role to play. Analysing one's Moon sign or Janam Rasi will reveal his love nature. We lay down here the effects of Moon in different signs in detail for Male and Female separately as this is of vital importance.

Moon in Signs

1. *In Aries*

   Males: Such persons are enthusiasts to some extent. Sometimes irritable and show fits of anger. One insists on his own way, disobedient to superiors, independent and self-reliant. Very spontaneous, optimistic, courageous, practical, of changeable nature, quick tempered, impulsive, aggressive and fond of travelling.

   In case Moon is afflicted, some danger of drowning and trouble through women. Makes one restless, rash and independent. Change of occupation.

   Females: Such women have a strong muscular body. Ambitious, quick tempered, angry mind, easily swayed by flattery, selfish. Married life is not usually happy. Suffers from mental worry, anxiety, brain disorder in latter part of life. Headaches and impaired eyesight. They are fond of work.

2. *In Taurus*

   Males: Quiet and impulsive, fond of friendship, love and marriage. Determined, ambitious, conventional, gain from father's business or inheritance. More sisters than brothers. One is sensuous and materialistic but social and of good disposition. Such natives are cheerful, kind hearted, helped through opposite sex, of good judgement, resourceful and encounter unexpected difficulties. Great liking for music and singing.

   When Moon is found afflicted, the native is passionate, prone to exaggerate and deaf to reasons and logic. Unfortunate through friends, love and sensitiveness.

   Females: Good looking with round face and beautiful well-proportioned body. Lustrous and beautiful eyes. Passive yet positive in thoughts and actions. Respectful to elders, fond of fine arts, stubborn, fond of good dishes, lazy and has love of luxury. Pleasure loving, fond of society, especially of opposite sex. Will marry and be well-looked after by her husband. Good housewife, educated and fond of travel. Loves good dresses and perfumes. Likes to be dominated by her husband.

3. *In Gemini*

Males: Agreeable, warm hearted, sympathetic, liberal mind, and of ingenious nature. Busy varied life. Reserved in personal and domestic matters. Changes emotions, dual nature, restless, seeking truth, lover of books and studies. One is of active mind, changes his residence, undertakes short journeys and is quite social. Lack of straightforwardness, one may have stepmother, brother or sister.

When Moon is afflicted, produces restlessness, confused mind, doubts and reverse results as shown above.

Females: Attractive, keen and intelligent face, beautiful and well-shaped body. Tendency to do many things at a time. Quick grasping power, talkative, romantic but not warm or affectionate. Helpful to their husbands. A good organiser but not a good housewife. Fond of reading and arts. Should avoid intoxicating drugs, liquors and medicines which will affect adversely.

4. *In Cancer*

Males: Fond of ease and comforts at home, attached to home and family. Friendly, social and changeable. Sensitive, generally are influenced. Imaginative and emotional. Become fortunate through directions of some competent man. Good ability for acting, mimicking, expressions of thoughts and music. Travel by water, insufficient self-control, economical.

An afflicted Moon indicates a shy, timid, fearful person without cause, not much care for his own or others' interests.

Females: Such ladies are of average height, round face, stoutness as age advances. Family women, greatly attached to home and family. Possessive, social, kind, religious, and respected. They are thrifty, of good character, loved by all and of pleasant disposition. As they age are subjected to rheumatic pains and aches and grow heavy.

5. *In Leo*

Males: Much vital force and moral courage. Helpful to weaker section, honest, sympathetic, generous and of open mind. Magnanimous, position of responsibility and prominence. Favourable for finances. Love of luxuries, pleasures, perfumes, dress etc. Favourite of opposite sex and a sincere lover. Unfavourable for a father. Good organising capacity, a leader among friends. Uplift of native socially and mentally. This position of Moon places him in a position of authority, trust, respect and responsibility and gives inspiration for great achievements.

When Moon is afflicted, it makes him proud, easily offended, conceited. One becomes fickle-minded and sensitive and experiences loss through women etc.

Females: Fair complexion, attractive, wide and generous features, big round eyes. They are generous, independent, leaders among women, jolly but easily offended or hurt and apt to be vindictive and jealous. Of fiery temper, fond of food and are religious. Joyous, sexy and craving for physical contacts, like to be away from madding crowds and prefer a solitary place. Sincere, frank, good married life on the whole. Wealthy, affectionate and passionate and as long as they love their partner, they do it intensely, otherwise will sever connections.

6. *In Virgo*

Males: Such persons have good intellectual power, good memory, trustworthy and fortunate through servants, easy going, irresolute, fond of science in general. Many friends, especially of opposite sex, of analytical mind and take many short journeys. Helpful to others, practical outlook of life. Changes in profession, secret sorrows through marriage. Such persons are fastidious, over discriminating, self-controlled.

When Moon is afflicted, bickerings become a mania, irritation and nervous overstrain. Troubles and separation in love and domestic life.

Females: Such ladies are beautiful and have a well-proportioned body and flashing eyes. Happy by nature but critical. Keep their homes fashionably. Sweet and persuasive in speech. Good orators, fond of music and dance. Hate vulgarity. Hard workers but get tired early. Confident in their views, but also offended easily. Quiet, attracted to opposite sex, and particularly to married men. Psychic and feel physical troubles.

7. *In Libra*

Males: This position inclines to union; partnership and general popularity. Fond of pleasures, society and amusements, company of the young opposite sex. Courteous, social, affectionate, agreeable, kind or equally sympathetic, warm hearted, kind in manners. Many friends. Early marriage.

Popular and attractive with opposite sex, gain through inheritance, lucky for house, property conveyance and graceful and commanding in appearance. Feelings will prove a good guide in all kinds of actions. Much of his fate and many events of life will come about through the association of other persons, greatly swayed and influenced by them. Tranquillity of thoughts and harmony in sensation is a must for success in life. Fond of agreement, concord and appreciations. Wealthy and attains good position in life.

As for marital relations, such persons enjoy good domestic life, love their homes and children. In case of differences with wives or beloveds, they maintain peace.

When Moon is afflicted troubled love affairs and afflicted domestic life and disappointments accrue. Crazy and wavering mind, delayed marriage and dependent.

Females: Libra-born ladies are oriental in appearance, dark magnetic eyes, beautiful, regular features, attractive and well-proportioned body. They are very social, orderly, sympathetic, very impulsive, neat, hasty in thoughts and actions. Affectionate, avoid hurting others or facing confrontations. They may be antagonistic but outwardly agreeable and insincere. Fond of education, and of independent career. Such ladies are married and make intelligent and helpful partners. Kidney and generative organs are weak.

Such ladies have delicate skin, beautiful breasts, and have a knack for choosing perfumes, dress and ornaments.

8. *In Scorpio*

Males: Firm, determined, self-reliant and conservative. They can withstand the battle of life alone with courage, energy and hard work. Averse to change, difficult to influence, and obstinate. They will become very revolutionary and changeable.

Sometimes they are irritable, angry and revengeful. Have many children. Not favourable for mother and her side of family. Position of Moon does not favour morality and may induce drinking, often cause coarseness in speech or manner and threaten some scandal to the native. Love of occult science.

Fond of pleasure, comforts and desires, cannot tolerate any restriction or opposition. Danger through voyages.

When Moon is afflicted, one has disharmony in married life and difficulties with opposite sex. Makes a person passionate, sensuous, partial and vindictive.

Famales: Scorpion Moon sign of ladies indicate plumpness and weight, dark or fair complexion, superfluous hair on body. Body is well-proportioned.

Such ladies are arrogant, proud, jealous and vindictive. Of loose and bad morals, excess drinking and other vices. Strong constitution and robust health. Shrewd, passionate, revengeful, can do anything and commit crimes connected with revenge. Fond of spices and hot food. Cold blooded and heartless. Unsympathetic. They have many secret friends and associates, may gain wealth through questionable means. Throat affliction and diseases of generative system are indicated.

9. *In Sagittarius*

Males: Argumentative, practical, determined, firm and self-confident. Have drive, gain and success. Fond of pleasures and fulfilment of desires. Energetic, courageous and positive. Forceful, independent and aggressive. Continual desire for knowledge, very sincere but secretive. Good vitality, leadership, fond of journeys, and sports.

Strong love nature and fond of pets. Religious belief. Inclination for mysticism, psychism and the occult. A good natural teacher or preacher, clairvoyance, tendency to dreams and somnabulism. Two or changeable occupations.

If Moon is afflicted, one is self-indulgent, unsteady, changeable and in subordination and reverse results of the above.

Females: Such girls have large forehead, muscular body, tall and well-proportioned body, bright eyes, charming appearance and graceful look.

They are religious, joyous, generous and lovable. Helpful to others, ambitious, helpful friends, healthy, do not have grudges, are generous and forgive those who hurt them. Fortunate and successful. Cooperative and hard workers. These women love life and get the most out of it. Artistic in their home and happy in life.

10. *In Capricorn*

Males: Such Moon renders the feelings strong and steadfast. Reliable, they are cautious in money matters, too cold and calculative and at times regardless of others' feelings. The native thirsts for moral and social advancement. Popular or notorious. If well aspected by Sun, respectable and prominent. A good administrator, ruler or leader. Opposition and loss through them.

If Moon is afflicted, separation of wife and partner, disharmony, difference of age, social position and possessions. Lack of creative energy, selfish, eccentric, chaotic, and inclined to upset things.

Females: Such ladies are slender, have a long face, are ambitious, and can be career women. Active, independent, argumentative, dogmatic manners and views. Fond of music, honest and truthful. Fond of opposite sex, they usually marry early.

11. *In Aquarius*

Males: Active, agreeable and courteous. Sympathetic, happy, optimistic, love of work, fond of the company of fine and good people. They go for political, educational and scientific work. One may be interested in astrology and occult sciences. Secret societies. Liking for the strange and curious, occasionally feel sorrows and may change through friends. Moon in Aquarius increases the imagination, intuition, and mental sensitiveness. Gain through inheritance.

When afflicted, indicates doubtful nature, laziness, self indulgence, one can be led astray easily. Unfavourable for marriage. Eyesight may suffer.

Females: Such girls are very beautiful, tall, oval face, magnetic and handsome appearance. It is so said that they are as beautiful as Moon.

Such damsels are brilliant, wealthy, acquire wealth and enjoy social status after marriage. Fickle-minded at times and odd in their behaviour. Imaginative, inventive, intuitive and inspirational. Self-respect, good reputation and of charitable nature. They love outdoor life and sports but sometimes they are wayward and vain. As regards health, they will suffer pain etc. in feet and lower limbs. A weak eyesight with age.

12. *In Pisces*

Males: The native is quiet, retiring and easy-going. Restless, fond of society and variety. Irresolute and not always to be depended upon. Such persons are restless, easily discouraged, meet obstacles, opposition and misfortune in life. Favours travelling by water. Liking for romance, but not favourable to love affairs. Very receptive, inspirational, suffers through misunderstanding. He should not exaggerate his feelings, obstacles make him dejected, easily discouraged and feels irresolute.

When Moon is afflicted, one is of doubtful nature, lazy, self-indulgent and one can be easily led astray.

Females: The girls with this Moon sign have a round, pleasant and affable face, puffy cheeks, large liquid eyes which are very prominent, and have a soft mouth.

Such ladies are emotional, dreamy, inactive, stubborn, and least provocative. Their eyes are full of sex and lust. They should avoid hurting others at any cost. They are modest, kind, courteous and lovable. Soft and good natured, nervous temperament but highly romantic. Fond of love, poetry and music. Helpful to the needy and can even sacrifice themselves for those in distress. Charitable nature. Gain from legacies and inheritance rather than from husband's wealth. The health will remain average.

Compatibility Table

The following table is a "Love Guide" or "Marriage Guide", according to Moon sign. It provides agreeable and disagreeable Moon signs of boy and girl. Moon sign either 3rd or 11th from the Moon sign of girl are considered good for boy. Similarly the girl's Moon sign which is 4th, 7th or 10th from the boy's Moon sign is quite favourable. These rules can also apply to Sun sign and also to Ascendant for boys and girls.

S.No.	Moon sign or Janam Rasi	Agreeable Moon sign	Disagreeable Moon sign
1.	Aries	Gemini, Cancer, Leo, Sagittarius Capricorn, Aquarius and Libra	Tauras, Virgo, Scorpio and Pisces.
2.	Taurus	Cancer, Leo, Virgo, Scorpio, Capricorn, Aquarius and Pisces	Gemini, Libra, Sagittarius and Arias
3.	Gemini	Leo, Virgo, Libra, Sagittarius, Aquarius, Pisces and Aries	Taurus, Cancer, Scorpio and Capricorn
4.	Cancer	Virgo, Libra, Scorpio, Capricorn, Pisces, Aries and Taurus	Leo, Sagittarius, Gemini and Aquarius
5.	Leo	Libra, Scorpio, Sagittarius, Taurus, Aries and Gemini	Virgo, Capricorn, Pisces and Cancer
6.	Virgo	Scorpio, Sagittarius, Capricorn, Pisces, Taurus, Gemini, Cancer	Libra, Leo, Aquarius and Aries
7.	Libra	Aquarius, Sagittarius, Capricorn, Aries, Gemini, and Leo	Pisces, Taurus, Virgo and Scorpio
8.	Scorpio	Aquarius, Cancer, Capricorn, Pisces, Taurus, Leo and Virgo	Aries, Gemini, Libra and Sagittarius
9.	Sagittarius	Aquarius, Pisces, Aries, Gemini, Leo, Virgo and Libra	Scorpio, Capricorn, Taurus and Cancer
10.	Capricorn	Pisces, Aries, Taurus, Cancer, Virgo, Libra and Scorpio	Aquarius, Gemini, Leo and Virgo
11.	Aquarius	Aries, Taurus, Gemini, Leo, Libra, Scorpio and Sagittarius	Cancer, Pisces, Capricorn and Virgo
12.	Pisces	Taurus, Gemini, Cancer, Virgo, Scorpio, Sagittarius and Capricorn	Aries, Leo, Libra and Aquarius

RETROGRADE PLANETS

As already studied in previous chapters, we now know that Sun, Moon, Mars, Venus and Saturn with Rahu and Ketu have striking bearings, and affect the life of man and woman in sex, marriage, compatibility, other social and domestic deeds. Sun and Moon are never retrograde whereas Rahu and Ketu are naturally always retrograde.

So we now study Retrograde planets and their effects on above aspects of life.

Mars Retrograde

Retrograde Mars causes woman to become frigid or go to extremes. There seems to be no middle course. Such a woman has sex-aversion even with her husband.

The women having retrograde Mars in their chart, bitterly complain that their husbands are after other women. They are not satisfied with their husbands in marital affairs, not because they are too sexy but because they themselves are averse to sexual relations as per their physical energy and vitality never rises to meet the challenge. They are against sex and turn the native to a homosexual.

Some woman frequently rebel against their own desires, try to stifle them, preferring to act, when they have to face tremendous odds, subconsciously seeking an excuse for the failure they anticipate.

Mars retrograde six to eight days, of course, that is sixty to eighty years in a horoscope progression. During its slow moving period, two weeks before and after retrogression, it indicates the effects for ladies.

Venus Retrograde

The effect of retrograde Venus is disastrous to the happy married life. If after a few years of marriage Venus turns slow and retrograde, the woman lacks in sex resulting in her husband turning to other women and married life becomes hell. As Venus grows slowly and retrograde, the man or woman feels impotent and becomes disinterested in sexual relations.

Ladies having Venus retrograde in their birth charts tend to become fastidious, of reserved habits. They are also inclined to unconventional love expressions, may renounce love for religion and become quite ceremonious.

But when Venus turns direct, the native assumes a personality, physical appearance, vigour attractive to the opposite sex etc. Venus seems to work alike in all signs when retrograde. It affects men particularly.

Mercury Retrograde

Persons with retrograde Mercury in their birth chart tend to think in terms of symbols and insights rather than facts and figures. The mind works more easily on the sub-conscious level, hence their insights into motivations are often uncanny and revealing. Such people are amazingly profound, creative, discovering possibilities which are more direct, obvious, practical. Such people talk to themselves and hum little tunes. They do not seem to hear other persons. They justify their actions with reasons they grasp after the matter is concluded.

It is always worthwhile listening to persons with Mercury retrograde. What they say may not apply to the matter in hand but is ultimately correct.

Jupiter Retrograde

Such persons often get success in other people's failures. They start at the point, where others become discouraged, and have unique ability to succeed in projects which have been abandoned. They are people who become surprised when they find opportunities are worked out with ease. Such people revive sick companies and uncover hidden assets etc. or in other words they do some remarkable jobs which cannot be done by others. In order to achieve their mental goal they prefer to bargain.

Saturn Retrograde

Persons with Saturn Retrograde in their birth charts do not like to be known in public, they find security in intellectuals or spirituals. They yield easily to external influences. They either appear shy, uneasy, introvert, lacking in self-assertion or attempt at times to cover this lapse with a pretext of arrogance. They feel alone, isolated, separated from their friends and are seldom understood. They are reserved.

LOVER'S GUIDE

This guide has been designed according to the entry of Sun into a zodiac sign as per Hindu astrology. Apart from general effects on males and females, each sign has been sub-divided further into three parts to narrow down the effects in a clearer way.

1. Aries Lover (April 13th-May 14th)

Males: This lover is extremely frank, enthusiastic in love, of practical views, lasting affection and demands your best at all times and does not hesitate to let you know when you are slipping. Adventure and freedom are the plus points of this lover. He is of a dominant nature and will be following so fast behind you that you won't go very far. Romantic, rash, passionate but a spendthrift.

Females: This lover is witty, intelligent, and independent. She expects her praise from you and expects good care. She will have the power to override and boss over you, can be aggressive but very romantic and sexy. Fiery in passions, and can be controlled with tact and patience as she wants freedom before and after marriage and you have to trust her because she will be faithful.

(a) *Born April 13th-22nd April*: The best guy for marriage and a family life, is he/she who has a urge for family tie-up and attachment to home. Less impulsive, most sensual of the Arien lovers and also of practical nature.

(b) *Born April 23rd-May 2nd*: Your lover has his/her own selected group of friends and requires much social stimulation from them. In addition he/she will go only so far in cooperating with your wishes, dominates and is in control.

(c) *Born May 3rd-May 14th*: More agreeable and companionable than most, getting a commitment from him/her is easy if you have proved to be dependable. In financial crisis this lover may sometimes even forget that love exists. They are fond of music etc. Ladies are aggressive.

2. Taurus Lover (May 15th-14th June)

Males: Your lover is devoted to you, reliable, generous and faithful. Sincere in love opposition and upsetting conditions. Not impulsive in love but responds well to kind treatment. A domestic bird.

Females: Your lover is of doubtful nature, anxious to lead a happy domestic life. Sincere in love and peace loving, social, affectionate and loving. When opposed, he becomes stubborn and unyielding. Usually secretive and reserved.

(a) *Born May 15th-May 23rd*: It may be difficult to get a commitment because love, sex and passions are more interesting if there is variety. Also this lover is so good with words that you feel you are the only love he/she has. Monetary concerns are not strong in this lover. Such ladies are extremely affectionate, but not lured by sex.

(b) *Born 24 May-2nd June*: Much quieter, more determined and stable than others. There is a depth to the emotional passions. He/she is best suited for a social and total commitment and has love relationship with one person. You can be more possessive with this lover. Ladies are level headed, seldom carried away desires of sex, are considerate and thoughtful.

(c) *Born 3rd June-14 June*: Your lover has usually two interests at the same time, due to the intense need for mental and social variety. It will be hard to get a permanent commitment from him and maintain your feelings. This lover could hurt your feelings. Ladies are self-disciplined, do not express desire, and they are loyal.

3. Gemini Lover (15th June-14th July)

Males: Your lover feels that variety is the spice of life. He makes quick friendship, finds faults with others and loses them, so he cannot find a permanent friendship. He is the most difficult lover to hold and keep. He cannot be understood easily. Calculating and cynical in love. Do not ask for any commitment from him. Best way to arouse him is to become disinterested in him yet friendly. He is quite impersonal.

Females: Your lover is intelligent and wants mental companionship. More interested in outside activities even after marriage. She cannot tolerate any opposition to her wishes and plans, cannot easily be imposed upon. If a situation arises she can leave you or the home.

(a) *Born 15th June-23rd June*: Emotions do not play much in the sex life of your lover, likes privacy and sweet moments of love. He/she is very sensitive, less talkative and outgoing. Likes company of intellectuals. A casual attitude may hide deep-seated worries or insecurities, love helps these ladies. They like witty and intelligent persons.

(b) *Born 24th June-3rd July*: Do not be fooled by the gentle manner and witty conversation of this lover, until you are totally sure of his/her sincerity. Learning new things are more important to him/her than home. Possessive, you will be expected to be loyal, even if he/she is not. Ladies like variety and music.

(c) *Born 4th June-14th July*: Lack of attention or not much affection will immediately hurt this lover's feelings. It seems that no matter how much love you bestow on him still there is something wanting in this lover's heart. This lover has an urge to settle and raise a family. He clings to relationship. Ladies are unpredictable and have unconventional attitude towards love, can be extremes. Emotions are not easily aroused.

4. Cancer Lovers (15th July-14th August)

Males: Life without romance is monotonous to your lover, yet loyal, sincere and affectionate in love, but undemonstrative in loyalty and sincerity. Once involved he is a sincere and ardent lover. Romantic and passionate. Difficult to understand, sensitive and secretive.

Ladies: Your lover is sincere, loyal and devoted, becomes moody at times. When neglected, overlooked or ignored becomes stubborn, determined and unyielding and may change the partner as she cannot tolerate this.

(a) *Born 15th July-24th July:* Friends are important and this lover has usually a following. He/she is more outgoing and generous than others but also can be demanding, preferring to rule the roost. Ladies are emotionally involved and are moody.

(b) *Born 25th July-3rd August:* Very sensitive, a little annoyance may compel your lover to change partners. Home and family are important, so love relations within family are preferred. If not satisfied emotionally they become moody and secretive. Ladies have strong, deep and aggressive attitude towards love.

(c) *Born 4th August-14th August:* Be sure that this lover is sexy, intelligent, fantastic and the best lover, then you should be willing to keep relations with him/her. There is a strong tendency to become vain, seeking flattery from others. Don't let their interesting connections influence you. Ladies have romance as a basic right. Dreaming or moody.

5. Leo Lovers (15th August-15th September)

Males: Yours is an ideal lover, romantic, fiery in passions but sincere and faithful in love. To show love publicly is below his dignity. Good-hearted. Fond of opposite sex and remains surrounded by ladies. It is safe to have commitments when once you have won his heart.

Females: They are ambitious and ideal, should not doubt their lovers. They have everlasting love but need to be kept under control. Popular in opposite sex, not selfish, very passionate and require self-control lest they go beyond limits, are of fixed ideas, dogmatic views and expect their word to be law.

(a) *Born 15th August-25th August*: This lover needs a more practical and mature sweetheart. He can be critical and exacting, expecting you to be at your best all the time. Since he may be more conservative, expects loyalty and love. Ladies have ardent and strong desires. They do not enjoy life without expression of love.

(b) *Born 26th August-4th September*: This lover is social and community oriented, requires your opinion all the time and often places you on a pedestal. He/she is much more generous and less fastidious. Modest but demanding.

(c) *Born 5th September-15th September*: Trust this lover if you want that someone should honestly help you in your practical affairs. Very shy, appears disinterested or aloof but the real cause is insecurity and uncertainty. Much efforts are needed to convince him/her. Ladies have strong desires and quick-responses.

6. Virgo Lover (16th September-15th October)

Males: They give more weight to intelligence than pleasure and romance. So you should have good reasons to pursue this lover, because he/she will insist on knowing the sincerity of your feelings. They are loyal lovers with a very romantic nature. This is only revealed to those they love. So courtship can be full of surprises.

Females: They are intelligent, wise, of accommodating nature and consider sex to be troublesome but if advised she can be an excellent sex companion. They should admire others as they want appreciation. Shy but not demonstrative in love. Passionate but have fault-finding nature.

(a) *Born 16th Sept.-25th Sept.*: This lover is strong and passionate. Keeps a sense of humour with him, which in turn can lead to a happier love life.

(b) *Born 26th Sept.-4th Oct.*: The lover wants more solitude, is practical and seeks perfection in you. The least discord will upset the balance, especially if it concerns anything romantic. You should impress on your lover that you need him/her in all phases of life.

(c) *Born 5th Oct.-15th Oct.*: Sometimes he can become selfish, he/she requires a devoted sweetheart who can indulge in extravagances. Can be a very diplomatic mate. Natural surroundings are best suited for this lover. Any tendency on your part to become temperamental or too pushy can scare this lover away. Ladies have romantic attitudes with a background of comforts and soft music etc.

7. Libra Lover (16th October-14th November)

Males: Most lovable lover for sex life being an expert in love affairs, sincere and affectionate. Your lover has charming manners, is dress and fashion conscious. and attracts opposite sex, his passions rise and die quickly. He has a compromising nature. You should be sophisticated, well groomed and tactful to enjoy most with him. He is a lazy lover unconcerned with the practical details of life.

Females: They are intelligent, tactful and wise. Passionate in nature. They love and adore their partner. Fond of dress, music, dance, restaurants, and clubs etc. Cannot be imposed upon. Emotional and extravagant, amiable, and ready to forgive and forget.

(a) *Born 16th Oct.-25th Oct.:* The extreme need for companionship as well as sexual satisfaction is deep. Your lover is shrewd, conservative and compromising. You will have to be practical and intellectually compatible in order to please. He/she will make demands gently, but firmly. Ladies enjoy the atmosphere of love, beauty, glamour, comforts and luxury.

(b) *Born Oct. 25th-3rd Nov.:* This lover demands friendship, companionship, and good intellectual compatibility from the sweetheart. He/she is willing to compromise and to continue love relations. This lover expects you to be available at all times, for love, work and other matters. Ladies are unpredictable. They are unconventional in love life.

(c) *Born Nov. 4th-14th Nov.:* The intensity, passion and jealousy are at peak in this lover. He may dominate, direct and try to influence your activities. If you dislike his/her independence, you better find another lover. Never say anything insulting and do not take it as an affront if your lover does so.

8. Scorpio Lovers (15th November-14th December)

Males: Rash in temperament but of adjustable nature. Intense, dynamic in romance and love, but of complex moods. Cannot tolerate any criticism. They should be given sympathy, good understanding and steady affection to enjoy sex and love life. Valiant and of fixed views.

Females: Ladies enjoy life if their partners show equally genuine affection and deep love. They suddenly lose their temper and pounce upon their spouse or lover without caring for his position, so why not avoid this to lead a harmonious life? They are very passionate and ardent in love.

(a) *Born Nov. 15th-Nov. 24th:* He/she is very independent and secretive. It would be easy for this lover to act like a playboy or playgirl, leading you to believe you are the only sweetheart. Optimism on your part, plus a less serious and possessive nature, makes this lover easier to live with. You will have to be tolerant of his friends and have desire for frequent trips. Ladies are extremes, either self disciplined or highly excessive.

(b) *Born Nov. 25th-4th Dec.:* This lover pays more attention to details, is more financially conservative, more possessive, less independent, and becomes melancholy quite easily. He/she will enjoy being alone with you. Ladies have deep emotions and sensuousness.

(c) *Born Dec. 5th-14th Dec.:* Your lover is very busy and has no time for dates and love. Travels, public obligations etc. do not allow him or her to fulfil the demands and commitments. Ladies have love for home and family life which form an integral part of their nature. This nature depends on their mood and feelings.

9. Sagittarius Lovers (Born 15th December-13th January)

Males: The love of freedom and independence can cause a problem if you are a jealous or a possessive lover. To make friendship with all is their basic trait. More interested in outdoor life than home and family life. The lover has expensive tastes, encompassing vast visions, with a belief in spontaneous luck. They love to travel for business, adventures or social work etc.

Females: They are fond of home and are non-interfering. Helpful to lover, calm, clever, polite and considerate. A reliable, intelligent, dutiful, obedient and pleasant person.

(a) *Born Dec. 15th-24th Dec.:* Less talkative and not spontaneous. This lover is so concerned with money and prestige that he/she seeks

friends or lovers who can further these interests. He is very
demonstrative behind closed doors. Ladies tend to be impulsive but it is
not likely to be their main interest in life. They like humour and joy.

(b) *Born Dec. 25th-3rd Jan.*: This lover is more extravagant, social,
spontaneous and impulsive. He requires constant affection. Chances are
that this lover enjoys travelling, philosophy and people, more money
and status.

(c) *Born Jan. 4th-13th Jan.*: This lover is pragmatic and exacting,
expecting you to help his/her career interests. He/she demands your
attention at all times. Such lovers are shallow lovers and are only
interested in social connections.

10. Capricorn Lovers (14th January-12th February)

Males: They are not emotional but slow and cautious, not bold in
approaching the opposite sex. Not demonstrative in love. So in case you
are looking for a dependable, sturdy and practical lover, he is the right
man. They are materialistic and often overcome their love and affection
for money. Public display of affection is not liked by them.

Females: They are much attached to home and family. Dutiful to
children. They do not display their love and hate any adverse publicity
or any hint of discard in their private life. They are conservatives.

(a) *Born Jan. 19th-23rd Jan.*: A very highly evolved person, using
his/her influence and talents to further the human cause. The idea of
brotherhood and political ties to it are of interest to this lover. There
may be conflict between his/her conservative views and eccentric novel
interests. You will have to be intellectually versaule, and willing to
experiment. Ladies have strong desires but are self-disciplined and have
patience.

(b) *Born Jan. 24th-1st Feb.*: He/she is devoted, can be fussy and
demanding of the mate. Too much of their time is spent outside the
home with friends. You get your aims fulfilled through demonstration
of love.

(c) *Born 2nd Feb.-12th Feb.*: This lover is so far ahead of times that
a conservative sweetheart could be constantly shocked, and
embarrassed by frank comments. Fighting for worthwhile causes can

often take him/her away from a love relationship. Ladies are neither impulsive nor rash.

11. Aquarius Lovers (13th February-12th March)

Males: Being intelligent they prefer an equally intelligent partner. This sexy, interesting and cosmopolitan lover may seldom be available to be with you alone. He is popular and very much in demand. Some of these lovers like love to be on a romantic and impersonal basis. They prefer permanent and strong attachments. They are cold and do not show love.

Females: They are unconventional. In case they find that their partner is not up to their standard they will not hesitate to satisfy themselves by changing the partner, otherwise will cooperate fully.

(a) *Born Feb.13th-22nd Feb.*: Adventure through companionship, requiring much affection and sympathy from you, can become a way of life. The lover has an easier time with marriage because he/she devotes much time to the sweetheart.

(b) *Born 23rd Feb.-3rd March.*: This lover has no possessiveness. There is a wide circle of friends and acquaintances. This lover requires him/her to be a friend or companion. In case they are not satisfied with the performance of their lover or partner, they will ditch him/her.

(c) *Born 4th March-12th March*: This lover is meek and mild when it comes to avoiding commitment. He/she is much more sensitive and intuitive than others. Physical beauty and sensuousness is strong in this lover and can lead to vanity. This lover reveals a gentle understanding and is a sympathetic sweetheart, who does not make too many demands. Ladies are romantic, impulsive, curious and are much attracted by the unusual and exotic experiences.

12. Pisces Lovers (13th March-12th April)

Males: They remain attracted to romantic life, prefer beauty of the partner and are intelligent. Suspicious by nature which kills their love but like flattery. They have their own dream world, one which is private and requires solitude. The need to be alone is very strong with them.

Females: Suspicious by nature, romantic and passionate. They are over-liberal and are very generous which should be avoided, so that they should not fall a victim to bad social elements and ruin their life. Sweet tempered, polite, social and can be led away by fancies. They love domestic life on the whole.

(a) *Born 13th March-22nd March*: Stronger, more sexually inclined and outgoing, this lover's security is very strong. If you hurt her/his feelings, anger results. Popular and active in society. Melancholy, seldom causes moodiness. Be flexible with this lover. Ladies are emotional and highly responsive.

(b) *Born 23rd March-1st April*: This lover is very strong and decisive when it comes to business, but when it comes to love he/she can be extremely susceptible to emotional pursuasions. What might appear to be a thick-skinned person on the outside, is a tender, loving, and devoted person really in love with love.

(c) *Born 2nd April-12th April*: Appearing tough and aggressive, emotional pulse is passionate and intense but commitments do not come easily. It is very difficult to hold on to this lover as he/she has a strong tendency to become bored. Ladies are aggressive and give full expression to their desires. But they should avoid brooding, self-pity, resentment, in order to achieve a healthy, outgoing attitude towards their life.

Sex Life Thermometers—Venus and Mars

A great scholar has said that sex alone is a mighty urge to actions, but its force is uncontrollable. When sex alone is a motive, a native may steal, cheat, or even commit murder or any other offence. But when emotions of love and sex are mixed, the result is calmness of purpose, poise, accuracy of judgement and balance, the same native will guide his actions with more serenity, balance and reactions. Love, romance and sex all are emotions. The emotions of sex is a virtue only when used intelligently and with discrimination.

Mars is a hot planet and Venus the brightest and coldest. When in a thermometer the temperature is zero, it is cold and when temperature is more, it becomes hot. Venus and Mars represent in the horoscope similar ideas of nature in males and females respectively. So these planets in a horoscope serve as a thermometer to read the marriage, sex and emotion temperatures.

Venus governs the sex life in male and Mars in female in the horoscope. Their strength, situation in sign and house and relations with other planets by conjunction or aspect are very important in judging the sex life of males or females.

When Venus is well placed, strong, unafflicted, it gives a balanced sex life. But when afflicted, it indicates adverse results. When Venus is in the house of Saturn, Mars, Rahu or Ketu or conjoined or aspected by any of these planets or has any relation with them in any way, the sex life of the male is either disturbed or abnormal or becomes unbalanced.

If Venus is in the sign of Mars or Saturn and is also aspected by Mars or Saturn, a person is sure to suffer from troubled sex life. Any benefic conjunction or aspect reduces the troubles. Influence of Mars or Rahu over Venus by association or aspect makes the native highly sexy. It also happens when Venus is in the house of malefic and is also devoid of any benefic aspect or conjunction.

Mars governs the sex life in a female. Its position, strength etc. in the horoscope are very important to analyse the sex life of a female. An unstinted Mars gives a normal and balanced sex life to the female. A strong Mars makes her sex conscious in early age. A weak Mars generally makes a woman cold in sex life. Afflicted Mars is always bad. When Mars is in malefic house, conjoined or aspected by malefic planet or planets that are in contrast in nature in a horoscope, it forewarns of disaster in life. All these lead to an unhappy married life. Affliction of Rahu to Mars is likely to increase her sex desire. It makes a woman highly sexy when Rahu is afflicted.

Moon represents mind, emotions and is important in a female's chart. A weak, afflicted Moon makes the woman weak-minded. She can also be easily influenced by the opposite sex, bringing her various troubles in life. But when Mars is also afflicted, she will lead an undesirable sex life. Sun has control over fame, reputation etc. and in a horoscope where Sun, Moon and Mars all are afflicted a woman/man leads a very miserable life.

So in the light of the above dictums we proceed further to analyse the sex life of males and females keeping in view Venus and Mars as there is not much difference between male and female horoscopes in the aspect of sex.

When Venus is afflicted in a birth chart it indicates amorous nature immoral life, rivalry, jealousy, unsmooth life, rash and violent actions, unpleasant domestic life, separation, divorce, ill reputation, plurality in sexual relations, sexy and questionable conduct etc.

In a male chart, fo, the purpose of marriage and sex, Venus is the planet governing marriage and sex life. Also rules over semen and genital organs. But plays too a vital role in a woman's chart.

In a female horoscope, for the purposes of marriage and sex, Mars is the planet governing marriage, life partner and sex life. Mars also rules over ovaries and female organs. Mars is predominantly responsible for menstrual flow and its duration is controlled by Moon.

Linking the Signs

This is a ready reckoner for checking the relations between two parties, whether they will remain happy or not. In case you do not know the date of birth of anyone, it does not matter. Check the sign in which the first letter of your name falls and compare it with the sign for the type of relations. Or in case you know Moon sign, Sun sign, ruling sign or Ascendant, you can check.

The term partner includes business partner, life partner, lover, beloved, friend, enemy or any other person in whose contact you come. A guide to various zodiac combnations will benefit the readers to check and analyse whether the contracts, partnership etc. will be established or not.

In our day-to-day life, we find that some close human relationships inspire a sublime degree of happiness, we like each other at first sight, or are immediately attracted; on the other hand they may lead to nothing but contact and acquaintance. In other cases we find conflict, unhappiness or we feel do not feel happy to see the other party for no apparent reasons. Astrology, the oldest science can supply many answers to the riddle.

All combinations of 12 signs are listed, giving a total of 78 pairs.

CHECKLIST

Sign	First Letter of your name indicating Moon sign	Sun Sign as per Hindu Astrology NARAYANA system
1. Aries	चू, चे, चो, ला, ली, लु, ले, लो, अ	13th April-14th May
2. Taurus	ई, उ, ए, औ, व, वी, बु, वे, वो, ब, बी, बू, बे, बो	15th May-14th June
3. Gemini	क, की, कु, के, को, घ, ङ, छ, ह	15th June-14th July
4. Cancer	ही, हु, हे, हो, डा, डी, डू, डे, डो	15th July-14th August
5. Leo	म, मी, मू, मे, मो, ट, टी, टु, टे	15thAug.-15th Sept.
6. Virgo	टो, प, पी, पु, पे, पो, ण, ठ	16th Sept.-15th Oct.
7. Libra	र, री, रू, रे, रो, त, ती, तू, ते	16th Oct.-14th Nov.
8. Scorpio	तो, न, नी, नु, ने, नो, य, यी, यु	15th Nov.-14th Dec
9. Sagittarius	ये, यो, भ, भी, भु, भे, घ, फ, ढ	15th Dec.-13th Jan.
10. Capricorn	भो, ज, जि, जू, जे, जो, ख, ख्वी, खू, खे, खो, ग, गी	14th Jan.-12th Feb.
11. Aquarius	गू, गे, गो, स, श, सी, सु, से, सो, द	13th Feb.-12th March
12. Pisces	दी, दू, दे, दो, थ, त्र, च, ची, झ	13th March-12th April

ZODIAC SIGNS

There are four elements of signs. Fiery signs are Aries, Leo and Sagittarius. Airy signs are Libra, Aquarius and Gemini. Watery signs are Cancer, Scorpio and Pisces. Earthy signs are Capricorn, Taurus and Virgo.

(i)   Fiery signs do not combine readily with watery or earthy signs.

(ii) Airy signs are compatible with air and fire.

(iii) Watery signs are compatible with water and earth, not with fire or air.

(iv) Earthy signs are not compatible with fire or air.

A writer has rightly said, "Yes, people who need people are the luckiest people in the world.....as long as they don't end up as star-crossed lovers. Some combinations are simply signposts to strife."

So on the basis of the above, we now provide the combination guide to Zodiac togetherness and tangents.

LINKING THE SIGNS

1. Aries

1. *With Aries:* Fire with a fire is a compatible combination, although it produces a volatile, exciting and sometimes stressful atmosphere, peace, quiet and relaxation will be difficult to achieve. If both people try to rule the roost, disputes and tension will result. When necessary, each will defend the other; your arch enemy—boredom—will seldom arise in this duo because you both like to be active.

2. *With Taurus*: Fire with earth is not an easy combination. Since the needs and nature of these signs are so different, there will be difficulties without compromise. Aries needs the stimulus of new enterprises or challenges but Taurus prefers quiet stability. Aries becomes impatient while the Taurus person has slowness and stay-put attitude.

3. *With Gemini*: Fire with air is agreeable and both generate a lively atmosphere, life is not boring. Gemini wits can match the Aries fighting spirit. You both enjoy variety, action, discovery and new things, so you should share your interests.

4. *With Cancer*: Fire with water can create problems unless you

search for a common ground. Cancer is sensitive and is often hurt by Aries's frank, sarcastic, abrupt or even abrasive ways. Aries does not appreciate Cancer's sentimentality and emotional moods.

5. *With Leo*: Fire with fire is a positive combination and provided you do not both try to be the boss, this can be a stimulating duo. Leo can appreciate the Aries drive and initiative while Aries is not overwhelmed by the big ideas, power and largeness of Leo. Both signs are outgoing, extrovert, warm and vibrant.

6. *With Virgo*: Fire is volatile and impetuous, whereas earth is practical, stable and self-controlled. There is a great contrast of temperaments here.

Aries cannot be bothered with the method, fuss and attention to details which comes so naturally to Virgo although Aries appreciates the results. Emotional natures differ so much that a good mental affinity is vital.

7. *With Libra*: Fire and air have natural affinity though they are opposite signs. They can repel as well as attract. If conflict arises, Aries triumphs while Libra becomes upset and leaves. Initially, there is often a strong physical or emotional attraction between these two.

8. *With Scorpio*: Fire with water creates a highly charged association. Mars rules over both signs, so there will be mutual appreciation of strength or capabilities or fierce competition. Aries does not suspect the secretive ways of Scorpio. Excellent for team work, if goals agree, but these signs will demand much of each other.

9. *With Sagittarius*: Fire with fire does not conflict. Both are independent, you must allow each other some freedom. Sagittarius encourages enthusiastic outlook and honesty. A fast tempo combination, so there is little peace and relaxation. Neither will tolerate the other being the boss.

10. *With Capricorn*: Fire and earth can be stressful. Capricorn likes to plan ahead and can play a waiting game. Aries acts immediately and hates to wait. Unless both people are willing to exercise tolerance, their extremely different viewpoints can bring tension or even bitterness. Capricorn often unwillingly squashes Aries.

11. *With Aquarius:* Fire and air is compatible. Both can generate tremendous power, so much will depend on whether it is used constructively. Aquarius will not dampen the initiative and independence of Aries, while Aries appreciates such friends. Aries loves anything new, so is interested in the Aquarian's off-beat ways. But if Aquarius becomes unpredictable at an appropriate time, Aries will be irritated and impatient.

12. *With Pisces:* Entirely different planets are ruling in nature. They are worlds apart and it will be difficult to find common grounds. Positive, active, Aries cannot fathom the nebulous, mysterious substance of Pisces who often irritates by appearing to be negative or indecisive.

2. Taurus

13. *With Taurus:* A stable, conservative and down-to-earth association and your relationship has enduring qualities. Leads association to lifestyle and to more adventurous type. When provoked, both can be jealous and possessive. Both are cautious of security. This team lacks dynamic initiative.

14. *With Gemini:* Your basic needs and motives are opposed. Gemini's love of constant change and variety can be upsetting for Taurus who likes to stay put. It will be an impossible mission if Taurus should try to possess Gemini.

15. *With Cancer:* They have much in common. Feelings, emotions and affections are important to both. Taurus appreciates the attention and protection which Cancer enjoys giving. Both are conservative, conflict can be caused by extremism or divergent interests. Common sense and logical discussions are the best antidotes when over-emotionalism develops.

16. *With Leo:* Unless both practise compromise, there will be conflict. Leo thrives on attention and affection. Taurus naturally dishes out. Taurus often tolerates being dominated by Leo. Until, one day, the worm turns. Leo's big ideas can be disturbing to the conservative Taurus.

17. *With Virgo:* Both are practical and cooperative, realistic and capable. However your emotional nature is not similar. Taurus being emotional and possessive can sometimes smoothen Virgo whose

feelings are much under control. Both desire material success and security.

18. *With Libra*: Bond will depend on feelings and affections or mutual appreciation of beauty and finer things of life. Harmony is their common point and they avoid provocation. Diplomatic Libra can tactfully manipulate stubborn Taurus. They both need your pleasures and luxuries.

19. *With Scorpio*: These are opposite signs. In love relationship, this factor often brings irresistible physical attraction initially but when it diminishes, the opposite happens unless both have more things in common. Both are jealous and possessive, so mutual trust is essential. Such intense feelings can sometimes bring about a turbulent love-hate friendship.

20. *With Sagittarius*: Taurus is one of the stable signs and you only feel secure when life is settled. Your nature is to stay put and be possessive. Your loved one may be at odds with Sagittarius as they need to feel free and independent. You are restless, enjoy things, far away places, travelling, and need plenty of -room both mentally and physically. Too much of this will prove very unsettling for Taurus. But true love can still manage to transcend all these differences.

21. *With Capricorn*: Both are security conscious. Taurus will always appreciate Capricorn's practical attitude, perseverance, realistic approach and ambition. Both are conservative, patient and willing to share responsibility. Neither believes in superficial pleasures, so life could be just too serious at times.

22. *With Aquarius*: These are two extremely determined signs which basically are separative in nature. Taurus will not understand his unpredictability and when Aquarius wants to be free and aloof he/she finds Taurus possessive. One has to give way. Aquarius has a natural desire to share affection with many people but Taurus is much more reserved with his feelings.

23. *With Pisces*: Lots of friendship, affection or love can be shared and they both appreciate beauty, pleasures and good things of life. Each can help the other because Taurus is practical whereas Pisces is a dreamer. When problems arise, clear thinking is clouded by too much emotion.

3. Gemini

24. *With Gemini*: This double dose of such highly strong, restless airy sign ensures, that life will never be dreamy or dull. The relationship can be lively, excitable, scatterbrained, gossipy, intellectually stimulating, full of change, variety, interest or nervous tension.

25. *With Cancer*: Gemini is mentally oriented whereas Cancer has emotions, so there is a marked contrast in nature. Variety, the spice of life to Gemini, can make Cancer feel unsettled. Cancer's sentimentality and emotionalism will not evoke a deep response in Gemini who, in turn never has time to fathom Cancer's moodiness. Gemini is always busy so that Cancer feels neglected.

26. *With Leo*: On mental and intellectual level both agree. Leo feels to be the centre of attraction but feels neglected when Gemini becomes absorbed elsewhere. Leo's desire to take control may overpower Gemini's free spirit. If both agree to let each other go his or her own way, this can be a sparkling combination.

27. *With Virgo:* A stimulating catalyst. Neither is over-emotional, both are practical in social, mental or business interests. Realistic and sympathetic. Virgo will not go along with Gemini's multitude of plans or scatterbrained ideas; Virgo concentrates more on one point.

28. *With Libra:* This creates a mutual appreciation of all that is refined, artistic, beautiful, sociable, interesting, informative. Gemini likes to communicate, so is happy to share with Libra who, in turn, is not satiated or complete when alone.

29. *With Scorpio:* Being opposite signs and also a stimulating combination, they repel and attract. Gemini is self contained, whereas Scorpio loves freedom and independence. Both are naturally busy and active people, so a mutual exchange comes easily to them.

30. *With Sagittarius:* Airy and fiery signs will maintain an interest on a mental or intellectual level. Sagittarius has a sense of independence, great love for freedom, restrictions on that are not tolerable. Both signs are opposite. Gemini and Sagittarius are not demonstrative, have an immense touch of love, quick wit, are generous and cheerful. Gemini lacks in concentration and quick decision which Sagittarius has. Both are fashionable, fond of society and has no chance of separation.

31. *With Capricorn*: Gemini can complement the wisdom and experience of Capricorn provided both are willing to communicate. Sometimes both have to agree or disagree. Capricorn is steady and controlled and Gemini fond of change. Capricorn does not always understand the highly strong, quicksilver ways of Gemini. Although very different, each can enrich the other with gifts etc.

32. *With Aquarius*: The lords of signs have very different natures with nice points. Gemini can accept a detached or unpredictable mood from Aquarius and is mentally stimulated both by Aquarian's originality and inventiveness. The unconventional and changeable quality of this friendship keeps it interesting.

33. *With Pisces*: A great difference in outlook and nature. Pisces is imaginative, dreamy and sensitive and lives by feelings, emotions, impression and intuition. Gemini is logical, factual and mentally oriented. However, both signs are reasonably adaptable and tolerant of other people's ideas, so although they will very seldom understand each other's driving force, they usually will accept it. Gemini is practical, quick and efficient whereas Pisces often dithers or is irritatingly indecisive.

4. Cancer

34. *With Cancer*: In this relation feelings and emotions will play a dominant role; this will bring great happiness, the reverse can also apply. Both are sympathetic and compassionate, so will help each other during troubles. Emotions can make clear thinking difficult, so some upsetting or muddled situations can occur when things go wrong.

35. *With Leo*: In spite of their different natures, there will be a strong bond. Cancer will often have to give way to the dominant Leo but Leo has a quality which makes Cancer's Moon shine more brightly. A Leo needs appreciation and attention which Cancer is happy to give.

36. *With Virgo*: Cancer is patient and willing to accept, Virgo will not be happy with quick and sloppy work. Virgo is too much of a perfectionist to do things in a hurry. Cancer is easily hurt and hypersensitive, so a Cancerian should not be criticised when he errs. Virgo is not too demonstrative, when it comes down to expressing feelings of love and affection.

37. *With Libra*: Cancer is easily hurt, unless the peace-loving Libra is provoked. It is unlikely to do anything to cause conflict; Libra will appreciate Cancer's natural desire to love, and protect but 'sometimes will impose on the Cancerian's desire to give. Due to excess of emotions of Cancer, Libra's balance between emotions and reasons may be disturbed.

38. *With Scorpio*: Both signs are related to feelings and emotions rather than facts and logic. When harmony prevails, this is the best duo, but if conflict arises, emotions go out of control and distort clear thinking. Each one is intuitive and can sense the wrong. So mutual trust is essential.

39. *With Sagittarius*: Both signs have great differences in nature. Without good communication Cancer will be isolated because Sagittarius is far too wayward and freedom-loving to be domesticated. Sagittarius is mentally, emotionally and physically independent which can make Cancer feel insecure. Both are generous in different ways; Cancer tends to cling, which causes Sagittarius to feel smothered or trapped.

40. *With Capricorn*: Without good communication this relationship will become dead. These are opposite signs in the Zodiac. Complementary and also a competitive relationship. Ambitious and success are the keynote. The sensitive Cancer will feel hurt or neglected. Cancer admires and benefits from Capricorn's sense of duty and responsibility but Capricorn sometime lacks the sentiments, warmth and loving care, which is very important to Cancer.

41. *With Aquarius*: Cancer's sensitive feelings and clinging emotions can disturb Aquarians who need time for independent and detached action. In a way Aquarius is universal rather than a personal lover who likes to share interests and affections with friends and humanity.

42. *With Pisces*: These signs are related to feelings, emotions, and intuition, which always have priority over logic, reason and analysis. Some practical necessities can become muddled or confused. They both feel things deeply, so each can evoke a sympathetic response in the other even without a word spoken. Both are very romantic and need to love and be loved.

5. Leo

43. *With Leo*: Both are strong willed; could be very good or very bad. If both are true there could be many chiefs and chiefdoms. Mutual give and take is very necessary. Alternatively, one will have to pay the second fiddle but which one? They can do everything if their goals and methods are alike.

44. *With Virgo*: Leo is an extrovert, rash and dominates whereas Virgo is modest, retiring and more inclined to be subservient. The success or failure depends on whose side the male or female is. In business, it is better for Leo to lead and Virgo to follow. Leo's ardent emotions can overwhelm self-controlled Virgo but the latter seldom actually shows it.

45. *With Libra*: Since both signs enjoy life, they will share a lot of happy times. Libra, who likes to keep things balanced, may think Leo to be lavish, extravagant or flamboyant. Leo likes to be the boss. Libra gets things done through tact and manipulation.

46. *With Scorpio*: These two powerfully strong-willed signs can prove excellent unless either tries to control or dominate the other. There is no limit to what they can achieve if their goals coincide and they strive together. Leo frank and open, will not understand Scorpio's secret, subtle manoeuvre and Leo often will disapprove of them.

47. *With Sagittarius*: This relation will work well, as both are optimistic, positive and take a broad viewpoint. Because both are frank, generous, and open hearted, they can be beneficial to one another. Leo will feel neglected or frets, if Sagittârius is too eager for freedom and independence.

48. *With Capricorn*: In the long run Leo could feel hemmed in or restricted by Capricorn who, in turn, will feel that Leo's ways are extravagant or demonstrative. Leo likes to live life to the full, whereas Capricorn being too cautious and conservative, likes to plan for the future. Capricorn, emotionally reserved and fairly undemonstrative, seldom realises that Leos will feel starved unless given lots of love, affection and appreciation.

49. *With Aquarius*: These signs are opposite to each other. There can be a strong initial attraction, which sometimes is transformed into equally strong opposition. You both have fixed opinions, strong determination and mind, so without compromise, there will be a clash of wills. Being Leo, you feel justified in claiming your partner's complete attention, whereas Aquarius likes to share interests, activities, ideals and affections with more than one person. Leo will not understand why Aquarius should be so unpredictable, detached and elusive and at the most unexpected times.

50. *With Pisces*: There is a great difference between the two. Leo is frank, open, an extrovert whereas Pisces has deep, mysterious, elusive qualities which are almost unfathomable to most people. Leo never knows what Pisces is made of, but the latter admires the strength of Leo. Pisces needs to be more organised and Leo is the one to do it. So if they live together in understanding this will be an excellent duo.

6. Virgo

51. *With Virgo*: Practical, realistic qualities, and each likes to have an organised routine, it is easy to fall into a rut. Neither will make impossible emotional demands on the other but each should avoid nagging or finding faults with the other.

52. *With Libra*: There is an apparent contract between them. They both are fastidious and seek some degree of perfection. Emotion and mind complement each other. Libra aims to achieve balance and beauty, so it is not likely to provoke the critical side of Virgo.

53. *With Scorpio*: Since both are practical and intelligent, this combination will work well. But emotionally these signs are worlds apart, Scorpio has intense feelings, burning desires and is often at the mercy of his or her own emotions, whereas Virgo believes in controlling them. Scorpio is demanding, so will appreciate Virgo's reliable conscientious qualities.

54. *With Sagittarius*: Virgo is methodical, careful, controlled and analytical. Fiery Sagittarius is impulsive, quick, independent and sometimes reckless and extravagant. Virgo is mentally equipped to specialise or concentrate on one thing at a time, handle small details and live in the present. Sagittarius is mentally broad-minded, optimistic, and always looks to the future. Self-expression of these signs flow through a different channel.

55. *With Capricorn*: They both appreciate the practical side of life and work. Both are conscientious, with a strong sense of duty and responsibility both are well matched for business and practical matters but there could be a lack of feelings, warm emotions and a romantic sparkle. Capricorn admires the systematic, methodical, self-contained and logical ways.

56. *With Aquarius*: Contrasts between the two signs. It emphasizes a mental and intellectual affinity rather than a deep emotional bond. Virgo is rational, intelligent, analytical and sometimes cool while Aquarius can be dispassionate, detached, uninvolved. Virgo is careful, self-controlled, and orthodox, but Aquarius can be unpredictable, temperamental and unconventional at times.

57. *With Pisces*: Virgo is the opposite sign of Pisces but both can complement each other. They see things with different eyes, each will always be a mystery to the other. Virgo is motivated by reason, analysis, facts and logic. Pisces is guided by feelings, emotions, intuition and that strange ability to sense what is what. Virgo brings method to Pisces's madness, romance, imagination. Pisces can add a touch of intangible magic to Virgo's life.

7. Libra

58. *With Libra*: Agreeable signs of beauty, peace, harmony and balance. Discord or conflict really upsets Libra, so each will avoid or leave unfinished anything likely to cause this. Both are easy-going and lack fighting spirit. So they do not make a progressive team. But are well matched in emotions, physical sex, elegance and have attractive and pleasing tastes.

59. *With Scorpio:* This relation can create physical, emotional and sexual attraction. However, Libra will find Scorpio more overwhelming at times. The secret of joy is to find a common point to share which gives pleasure and satisfaction to both. There is a mutual attraction between Libra's charming allure and Scorpio's sex appeal.

60. *With Sagittarius*: This union increases the qualities of love, success, happiness and ability to enjoy life. Although Libra needs to share things with someone special he is tactful enough to allow Sagittarius that much love, freedom and independence. Sagittarius is generous to allow Libra to indulge in little pleasures and luxuries.

61. *With Copricorn*: Cannot easily combine as there should be some common purpose or destiny to form long term association. Capricorns are not demonstrative and do not openly indicate warmth of love and affection which Libra needs. Libra enjoys ease, luxury and self-indulgence. Capricorn takes life seriously, shoulders responsibility and can cope with austerity much better than Libra. Capricorn should remember that sharing love, affection and beautiful things is as vital to Libra as food and water.

62. *With Aquarius*: They can share the pleasures together because Libra is the epitome of a personal lover whereas Aquarius is the universal lover, who needs to share the interest and affection with others. When Aquarius becomes aloof or unpredictable, Libra uses tact and diplomacy rather than anger to handle the situation. Neither of them will make impossible demands on the other. If Aquarius is allowed freedom by Libra, it can be an excellent union.

63. *With Pisces*: Although Libra is affectionate and Pisces of a different nature, yet there can be an affinity because both appreciate beauty, entertainment, arts, harmony, love, affection, gentleness and the magic of romance. Libra will help Pisces in moments of confusion, indecision and to be impartial.

8. Scorpio

64. *With Scorpio*: This double combination of emotionals strengthen strong feelings, desires, emotions and passions which both have. So with great desire and purpose they can achieve great things. If not, violent clashes are likely. There is a touch of both the saint and the devil in this combination or union.

65. *With Sagittarius*: Unless Scorpio compromises, the relation will create problems. Sagittarius's love of independence and free will arouses Scorpio's jealousy as he wants to possess, which is denied. Scorpio demands much of both self and others but Sagittarius will rebel against domination.

66. *With Capricorn*: Neither of them expects life to be an easy road full of fun and games. Both can be dedicated, determined and hard working. In serious and practical matters, they make a good team if their goals are the same. When conflict arises, they can be deadly enemies. Since neither of them readily gives up, serious rifts will not be easily or quickly resolved between the two.

67. *With Aquarius*: Both strong willed and determined, so if they can channel their combined forces into a common goal, great achievements are possible. Scorpio is intensely emotional and naturally passionate whereas Aquarius likes to feel free to share interests with many people. If Scorpio dominates there can be a clash, if the rift becomes serious Aquarius can separate quickly. Scorpio takes love as an intensely personal matter whereas Aquarius treats it as universal love, unless this difference is understood clearly between the two, Scorpio will feel that Aquarius is too impersonal and detached and their combination will not flourish.

68. *With Pisces*: The relation is magnetic in attraction, will generate an intensely emotional relationship. Scorpio dominates over others, Pisces, outwardly submissive, deviously manoeuvres. Pisces can soothe the inner tension, compelling desires and compulsive yearning within Scorpio. Each intuitively senses the other's moods, needs, fears and faults. When things go wrong an overabundance of emotion will cloud the issue and mar settlements.

9. Sagittarius

69. *With Sagittarius*: This team of Sagittarius with Sagittarius is active, enthusiastic, and optimistic—a lively team. Together they generate an atmosphere of restless activity and excitement, so that life will move fast. Both like freedom and independence, so unless they pull together and constantly reinforce the partnership there is a chance they will drift apart. Monetary and too many ties are their enemies.

70. *With Capricorn*: There is a marked contrast in this relation. Independent, freedom-loving Sagittarius will not take kindly to being repressed or restricted by Capricorn, who in turn, will not understand Sagittarian's inner longings, high ideals and impossible dreams. If they can bridge the gap and achieve a happy relationship, each will certainly benefit in the long term.

71. *With Aquarius*: There is a strong affinity between a Sagitarrian and an Aquarian. Each makes a strong impact on the other and also is willing to leave the other alone when necessary. Both have an independent streak and need freedom. They will attract many people and share the resulting pleasures and reciprocal benefits.

72. *With Pisces*: These relations are full of complexities and presents a multitude of possibilities. Some compatibility will be found in mutual appreciation, religion, mysticism, travels, charitable causes or other lofty ideas. Pisces's vivid imagination probably will conjure up the worst picture when Sagittarius feels the need to be independent. In spite of his good qualities, a Sagittarius lacks the softness and tender loving care essential for Pisces. The Piscean tendency to be indecisive, impractical and disorganised may exasperate Sagittarius who is basically active, impulsive and positive and likes to get things done quickly and efficiently.

10. Capricorn

73. *With Capricorn*: This combination multiplies a Capricornian's cautious, conservative, realistic approach to life. With a common goal, their ambitions and perseverance will ensure success. However, if one tries to use the other for selfish ends, it can lead to much bitterness and resentment. Outsiders who are more adventurous and relaxed are likely to find this duo too serious and formal.

74. *With Aquarius*: The relationship will be subject to changes of moods, routine and attitudes. Many personal readjustments will have to be made on both sides although these may not be easy to achieve because Aquarius is independent and stubborn about personal ideas while Capricorn can never fathom why Aquarius sometimes becomes unpredictable and capricious. This behaviour undermines Capricorn's desire for stability and security.

75. *With Pisces*: These signs complement each other. Pisces finds it easy to amalgamate and can adapt to people and situations which are safe and secure. Capricorn is the epitome of safety and security. Pisces is intensely sensitive, emotional, romantic and sentimental, so may feel sad or hurt when Capricorn hides his/her true feelings. Pisces is not one with aggressively competitive signs, so offers no apparent threat to Capricorn's ambitious and long range plans to climb the ladder of success. Capricorn's sense of management and excellent practical abilities will help to shelter the sensitive Pisces from some of the harsh realities of life.

11. Aquarius

76. *With Aquarius*: Much will depend on which of the many facets

of this sign each person reflects, but sooner or later, unusual, surprising, changeable or disruptive conditions will affect the partnership.

77. *With Pisces*: An unusual combination. Both are different from most people and feel sometimes a misfit except with other Aquarians and Pisceans. There will be at least two sides to the combination, firstly, the superficial layers of association appear to be quite ordinary and normal; secondly the unseen, hidden interplay of psychological forces make an obscure and highly complex relationship.

12. Pisces

78. *With Pisces*: In this relationship feelings, emotions, intuition, daydreams are in the fore and take precedence over logical and rational analysis. Each has his own private and secret world, senses things about people. Both can become muddled, disorganised, indecisive and in a dither, so there will be periods when time is wasted and confusion reigns in practical matters. Because they are so emotional and sentimental they cry when happy or sad.

How Opposite Signs Attract

So far we have studied many aspects of personal relations but a queer situation arises when two opposite signs come into contact and form relations. We have analysed this point in a most lucid way.

It is commonly said that opposite signs cannot marry each other or cannot enter into partnership as they create disharmony, misunderstanding and bitterness. These views are not correct.

In our view opposite signs help each other in marriage and business partnership. The deficiencies of one which have been supplemented and covered by the other sign can represent an ideal state. These views are supported by the well known Scientific Law, that *opposite poles attract, whereas similar poles repulse.*

There can be six such combinations. The signs relate to Sun sign. Ascending signs or Moon signs are dealt with in detail.

Aries-Libra

Aries indicates leadership, whereas Libra denotes cooperation and their combination can lead to an excellent partnership. Aries has ego, whereas Libra has a basic instinct of harmony. Aries is rash, a hard worker, energetic, very active and can withstand the oddities of life and is egoistic. This attitude of egoism and rashness generally does not pay in the long run in modern society but with the partnership of Libra, who has the basic nature of love, provides a way to strive through, creating a lovely and graceful private world. Libra enables Arians to go ahead successfully through hardwork while relaxing also. So the gap created by one is filled by the other if they join hands.

Such people can immediately and easily resolve their differences if any, because both are good orators and can discuss subjects well and can reach a correct decision.

Both signs indicate intelligence, diplomacy. They are practical and do not believe in postponing things. Their frankness and enthusiastic nature can further cement their ties and relations. Both want freedom and cannot be imposed upon, so they can adjust better with each other. Harmonious relations with all is their common point.

Arian husbands are very desirable partners. Usually they select beautiful and clever wives. Generous and beautiful, romantic but spendthrifts, rash and passionate. The *Arian ladies* are witty, intelligent and independent. Zealous, proud and always talk high of their family and domestic environments. A good host, but the Arian lady likes to be well looked after by her husband. They love to be admired and can be controlled with tact and patience.

On the other hand *Libra husbands* are cheerful, romantic, passionate and of adjusting nature. Accommodative, they take care of the family and their comforts. Good, expressive in love, want equal response from wife. The *Libra ladies* are beautiful, intelligent, tactful and wise, peace-loving, sexy and passionate, fond of dance, music, restaurant, club and societies. Peaceful, diplomatic and generous. Emotional, extravagant, amiable, ready to forgive and forget.

Taurus-Scorpio

Taurus persons are perverse whereas Scorpions have patience. Both are determined, obstinate and power ambitious, yet social and affectionate. Both will not stop at anything if angry but they are steady workers. So they will understand each other better than anyone else will.

Both have the magnetic power to attract others, fond of opposite sex and enjoy good health. Scorpions are good detectives and can prove useful to Taurus their power of intuition, mysteries and occult can strengthen the mutual relations to a greater extent than otherwise. In case of any misunderstanding both will hold grudges for a long time but will ultimately forget and forgive. Scorpions believe in evolution and revolution.

The *Taurus husbands* are devoted to their wives, adore them and are faithful. They do not neglect the home, wife and children. They like their wives to be well dressed, attractive and pleasing. *Taurus ladies* are good wives and mothers, reserved and calm. Anxious to lead a happy domestic life, be gentle and peace loving. Sincere, not hasty but dutiful. Divorce is rare with them.

The *Scorpio husbands* are rash in temperament but of adjustable nature. They adore their wives. Care more for prestige and family honour. *Scorpio lady* enjoys life if partner cooperates, has love and deep affection. Of adjustable nature, hard worker, suddenly loses temper and is very passionate.

Such mixed combinations produce excellent couples.

Gemini-Sagittarius

Both are not demonstrative, have immense love, quick wit, are humane, generous, cheerful and shy. During troubled times they are at their best.

No one can do things more successfully and gracefully than Geminians. They lack in concentration and quick decision which weakness is removed by Sagittarians. So the union lasts as they love each other and are loving. Both are fashionable, sociable and adaptable to all circumstances. Fond of society and having many more common traits, have no chance of separation, they even become zealous when they feel that their relationship is being threatened.

They enjoy life to the full. Both love the opposite sex. No doubt Sagittarius flares up quickly which lasts for a short time but to him home life is more important than anything else. *Sagittarius ladies* do not interfere in their husbands' affairs unless asked for and are adjustable in nature. They are intelligent, cannot tolerate any resentment by the partner. Similar is the case with husbands dominated by these signs.

Cancer-Capricorn

This is a happy blending of attachment and detachment. Both like a quiet and domestic atmosphere. Such persons form an ideal relationship and have complementary natures. They are emotionally insecure, clinging to each other rather. Capricorns are not emotional, but slow and cautious are not bold and rash and never take a lead. They take a long time to choose their partner and are undemonstrative in love and romance.

On the other hand Cancerians lead a monotonous life without romance, are loyal, sincere, and affectionate but lack in expressing their loyalty and sincerity to the partners, are honest and very true. They love their home and family life. A good parent and cares for the children.

Both husbands and ladies are sincere, loyal and devoted to their partners and form an ideal combination for marriage and friendship. They will not go in for conventional or unconventional relations or marriage but will have permanent ties.

Leo-Aquarius

This is a combination of personality versus collectivity, truly unconventional, even controversial but an excellent one. They love secretly. Remain united but do not cling to one another or stifle each other. Most cooperative with each other. Their home remains a place of laughter, joy and security.

Comparing the traits of both, Leonians are independent, rash in temper, faithful, fond of the opposite sex, of commanding and bossing nature, dominating. Have great affection for the opposite sex. Frank, warm hearted, cannot tolerate any restriction. Husbands love home, wife and children. *Leonian lady* is ambitious and ideal. Manages her home ideally, commands social and prominent position, is affectionate and a good wife.

On the other hand Aquarians are intelligent, have good memory, good concentration, self-controlled, humane and impersonal. Constant in friendship, strong in likes and dislikes. Social but choosy about friends. Husbands pay less attention to wife and family, are generous and sympathetic. Ladies are unconventional, want satisfaction and cooperation from partner, share responsibilities, work and duties.

Such a combination produces a happy couple.

Virgo-Pisces

A happy combination of discipline and tolerance. Relations may be unconventional. Virgos are methodical, active in mind, fond of learning, pragmatic approach to problems. Nervous and lacking in decision and self-confidence. Frank and expressive eyes. Fond of peace and domestic life. Fault finding nature, they love passion. Shy and not demonstrative in love.

The Pisceans are quick in understanding, inspirational, easy going, passionate, affectionate and charitable. As husbands, they lead a romantic life, affectionate, full of love but of suspicious nature. Remain attracted to the opposite sex throughout life. Very helpful and maintain harmony. *Piscean ladies* are beautiful, romantic and passionate, over liberal, and have unbounded generosity. Of sweet temper, very sociable and polite. They love domestic life.

Both cherish hopes. So their union is likely to not only survive, but prosper long after others have dissolved.

Ideal Match, Lucky Numbers and Colours

To sum up the whole discussion, we now finally provide for you, your ideal match signs, lucky numbers, days, colour and day of fast for your guidance and benefits in a tabulated and ready-reckoner form.

Sign	Ideal Match Signs	Lucky days	Numbers +ve -ve		Colours	Day of fast
1	2	3	4		5	6
1. Aries	Leo, Libra, Sagittarius	Tues, Sat, Fri, Mon, Sunday	9,1,4 8,2,3,5,	6,7	Red, yellow, copper, golden	Tuesday
2. Taurus	Virgo, Capricorn,	Fri, Wed,	2,8,7,9,	5	Pink, green	Friday
	Cancer Scorpio and Pisces	Sat, Monday	1,3,4,6,		White	
3. Gemini	Libra, Aquarius,	Mon, Thurs,	7,3,5,6,	4,8	Yellow, purple blue, green	FullMoonday
	Aries and Leo	Wed, Friday	9,1,2		and pink	
4. Cancer	Cancer, Scorpio,	Sun, Fri, Thursday	4,6,8,1	3,5,	White, cream	Monday
	Pisces	Mon, Tues Thursday	2,7,9		Red, yellow	

1	2	3	4	5	6
5. Leo	Aries, Sagittarius	Sun, Tues,	1,4,5,9, 2,7,8	Orange, red	Monday
	Gemini, Libra Aquarius	Wed, Thurs, Friday	6,3	Green	
6. Virgo	Taurus, Corpricom,	Wed, Fri,	2,3,5,6 1,8	Yellow, white,	Friday
	Cancer, Scorpio	Mon, Tuesday	7,4,9	emerald, green	
7. Libra	Gemini, Aquarius, Aries	Sun, Mon,	1,2,4,7 5,6,3,9	Orange, white,	Tuesday
	Taurus, except Cancer and Capricom. All other signs.	Sat, Tues, Wednesday	8	Red	
8. Scorpio	Scorpio, Pisces, Cancer	Sun, Mon,	3,9,4, 5,6,8	Yellow, red	Tuesday
	Virgo, Taurus, Capricom	Tues, Fri, Thursday	1,2,7	Orange, cream	
9. Sagitta-rius	Sagittarius, Gemini, Leo, Aries, Libra, Aquarius days	Wed, Fri, Thur, Sun	6,3,9,8 2,7,9 1,4	White, cream Green, orange light blue	Thursday
10. Capri-corn	Scorpio, Cancer Pisces	Fri, Tues, Sat, Wed	6,8,9 3 7,5,4 2,1	White, black, red, blue	Saturday
11. Aqua-rius	Gemini, Libra	Fri. Thurs. Tue, Monday	3,9,2 1,4,5,8 7,6	Yellow, rea White, cream	Saturday
12. Pisces	Virgo, Cancer	Sun, Tues, Thursday	1,4,3,9 8 7,5,6.2	Red, yellow Rose, orange	Thursday

6

FINANCE, PROPERTY, CONVEYANCE, CHILDREN AND TRAVELS

FINANCE

In a birth chart yogas tend to show the degree of goodness or adversity or richness or poverty during his life. Yogas for richness are called Dhan yogas and others are known as Arishta yogas for poverty or misfortune.

Six positions of established relationships between planets are:

1. Conjunction
2. Exchange of houses (Parivartana).
3. Mutual aspect
4. Two planets aspecting each other.
5. Position in mutual kendras and trikonas.
6. Planets occupying own houses or any one of the Shodasa Varga.

In addition to yogas, there are houses involved for Finances. 2nd house is for earning, inflow of money, whereas 11th house is for saving or accumulation of money. 12th house is for expenditure.

Yogas for Richness

1. Any two of the following seven houses, viz. Lagna, 2nd, 4th, 5th, 9th, 10th and 11th, related to one another either by combination, aspect or exchange of places, may confer wealth on the native. These are common to both sexes.

2. It must be remembered, that yogas formed by the following house lords will be much more effective and productive than any other combinations or relations among other lords aspected by benefic.

1. The lords of Lagna and 2nd house.

2. Lagna lord and 11th house lords.
3. The lords of 2nd and 11th houses.
4. The lords of 9th and 11th houses.
5. The lords of 10th and 11th houses.
6. The lords of 5th and 11th houses.
7. The lords of 2nd and 9th houses.

Example: In the horoscope of Leo Lagna, mark the conjunction, aspects etc. and check the results.

In this chart Lagna is aspected by the powerful Jupiter. 10th house lord and 11th house lord are in 3rd house aspected by Jupiter. Lords of 9th and 11th aspect each other without any malefic aspects. Also lords of 1st and 9th are in aspect.

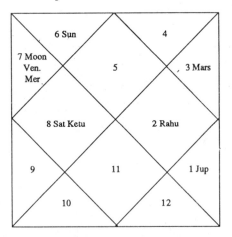

The native is blessed with all comforts of life by Lord Shiva. Other yogas are Gajkesari yoga, Karak yoga and Amala yoga.

3. The yogas will not be effective until the Lagna lord and 9th house lords are strong and well placed. These houses should also be occupied by favourable planets or house lords to help the native to get finances.

4. If 9th house lord is posited in any kendra or kona (trine house) house from Lagna or is exalted, in own house or in good house, the native becomes rich, highly qualified and efficient. (In the above chart 9th lord Mars is in 11th house where Mars is treated auspiciously.)

5. If 10th lord is in 10th, 5th, 2nd or 9th house.

6. Lord of 10th in 9th termed as "kshetra simhasan yoga" makes a man great and rich.

7. Saturn and Mercury conjoined in 2nd.

8. If powerful Mercury, Venus and Jupiter occupy Lagna, 2nd or 12th house.

9. If Moon in 2nd, Sun in 12th and both are aspected by benefic.

10. In case of Leo Lagna if 2nd house is posited with Venus, Mars, Saturn and Rahu, one may be very rich.

There are more yogas which may be referred to in author's other books.

Poverty

If the planets forming Dhan yogas are malefic due to position, in unfavourable houses or aspect or conjunction with malefic planets the native may suffer poverty. This is a general rule. The malefic effects may be modified or decreased due to aspect or conjunction etc. with favourable planets or in houses.

The yogas causing poverty are termed as Daridra yoga, Hradha yoga, Fanimukha yoga, Hutasana yoga, Kemadruma yoga, Lolati yoga, Sula yoga, Sarpa yoga, Dur yoga or Byaghratunda yoga etc.

Finance Houses and Lords

In Hindu Astrology houses 1, 2, 4, 5, 7, 9, 10 and 11 are termed good, benefic or auspicious houses so far as finances are concerned. If the lords of these houses are strong by house position or sign position or by aspect or by conjunction position etc., they give rise to good results in regard to the house over which they have lordship. In this connection, the house in which the mooltrikona signs of the planets fall should be taken as the house of which the planets are for mainly in evidence. The mooltrikona signs of the planets are for Sun, Moon, Mars, Mercury, Jupiter, Venus and Saturn as 5, 2, 1, 6, 9, 7, 11 respectively. If however, such planets are weak by house position efc. they will give bad results, even though they are lords of good houses. If lords of evil houses, viz. 3, 6, 8, 12 are strong they increase the evils of horoscope, i.e. poverty, debts etc. If on the other hand, they are weak and afflicted without any good influence, they destroy the evil in the horoscope and confer great riches and affluence. In the last case, it constitutes what is called "Vipreet Raj Yoga", i.e. yoga arising out of the weak position of bad planets.

Also if 3rd house lord occupies 8th house and is under the aspect, conjunction of natural malefics lords of 6th and 12th houses and is devoid of any influence, association or aspect of natural benefic planets, the configuration constitutes "Vipreet Raj Yoga" which confers extraordinary riches on the native.

The reason is that 3rd house is a bad house, if its lord is in 6th house from 3rd or in 8th house it will harm the prospects of 3rd house, which will suffer all the more under other malefic influences referred to above.

Refer to the horoscope for more clarification of Vipreet Raj Yoga

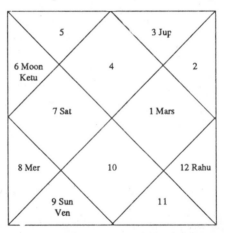

Raj yoga is of two kinds—Direct Raj Yoga and Vipreet Raj Yoga or Reverse Raj Yoga, which is of course conducive to much wealth. When the lords of benefic houses are such as those of kendras, and trines are in mutual relations by aspect, conjunction etc. and are strong, the yoga is created and is called Direct Vipreet Raj Yoga which is of course conducive to much wealth. But when lords of evil houses are in mutual relations, weak and afflicted exclusively by malefic planets, this weakness removes the evil effects of the evil houses over which they have lordship, and in turn the native gains much more than he does by having a Direct Raj Yoga during the dasa of these planets.

Here we provide general guidelines for finances for various signs. However, these can be modified as per birth chart.

1. Aries

Arians are not meant for amassing wealth in spite of their strong desire. They are extravagant and lose money through impulsive actions and rash investments. Evil or malefic planets if posited in Aries, indicate that they start in a flash and end in a crash. Their budget always remains unbalanced. They should think calmly and seriously before taking any action.

2. Taurus

Taurus persons being economical will accumulate and hoard money and never squander unnecessarily. Gambling nature is also indicated, is of materialistic mind, will get money from others, is practical and will rise gradually, and will take chances and will risk money.

3. Gemini

There will be lot of changes in life. They will enjoy life with good fortune and also suffer continuous misfortune, experiencing both privation and plenty. They will bring about their downfall by their own actions.

4. Cancer

Cancerians are very careful with money; being honest, they cannot tolerate any dishonesty. Accumulation of money through their hard work. Fortunate in finances.

5. Leo

Leos are generally fortunate and have sufficient resources. They are spendthrifts, their bank position will deteriorate as age advances. In gambling and speculation, generally lucky but these should avoided. Being liberal and generous are helpful to everybody and feel proud. Pleasures may lead to loss and trouble in old age if they do not control them.

6. Vrigo

Hard work will pay dividends and bring them to the top. Being of commercial nature, careful with money. Return of investment will be poor. If lord of 6th Saturn is exalted and has good aspects it denotes good fortune.

7. Libra

Some Librans excel over other people in matters of finance and good conveyance. They are extravagant, spend on luxuries, dress, etc. They are liberal and generous with donations for good causes.

8. Scorpio

They are lucky in wealth, gain through speculations, are blessed with money, vehicles, a good position in service or business. They are extravagant. Their income will be substantial as they know how to earn and make money.

9. Sagittarius

Sagittarians face frequent changes. They are rich and enjoy full comforts of life, they have gains without pains. If Jupiter is not afflicted, politics will prove lucky.

10. Capricorn

They are desirous of name, fame, money and reputation. Will work continuously to gain success. They do not miss any chance or opportunity and do not speculate. They will have enough money and comforts of life but should not expect a windfall.

11. Aquarius

Honours and money come to them without seeking. They are both fortunate and unfortunate.

12. Pisces

They have good business ability and are endowed with power and wealth. They do not depend on others. They have plurality of interests, are helpful to the needy. Must keep money for old age.

PROPERTY

Fourth house of the Zodiac ruled by Moon is significator of property (immovable), mother, conveyance, land, family happiness, inheritance, residence and garden etc. If 4th house, its lord and Moon—all emotional factors—alongwith other "intellectual" factors such as 5th house, its lord and first house, its lord and Mercury are all weak and afflicted by malefic planets, the native becomes mentally weak and in severe cases a lunatic.

Apart from indications as mentioned above, fourth house, its lord and Moon can be judged in many other ways such as, if Moon is lord of the 4th house and there is on the Moon an exclusive influence of Rahu, it shows a sort of phobia or fear in the mind and in severe cases one suffers from fits and swoons.

Like other characteristics property and conveyance are also indicated by this house.

Immovable Property

If 4th house and its lord are strong and Saturn has a link by association or aspect with 4th house as well as by the Lagna lord, the native owns much property. He may also earn through agricultural, farming, rent, sale of property etc. or if 4th and 10th lords join in kendra with Saturn also angular or in good Vargas. Also if in a birth chart a debilitated Jupiter sign is posited in 4th house, one acquires landed property.

TRANSIT: When Jupiter transits in 4th house or 10th house, the native acquires landed property whatever be the sign.

Example 1. In the horoscope Jupiter in 4th house is of debilitated sign. The lady, in spite of the fact that 4th lord Saturn is aspected by Ketu, has good landed property, two good houses.

During transit when Jupiter transitted in 4th house in 1985, she started construction of house in March, 1985. This forecast was given to her in 1982 by this author. Secondly transit of Jupiter in Taurus in 1988 aspecting 4th house is again responsible for constructing her second house.

2. In the horoscope, the native purchased the property when Jupiter transitted in 4th house in 1983 in the month of November.

Secondly, when in April 1956 when Jupiter was in transit in 12th house, in his exalted sign, aspecting 4th house, the native started the construction of his house.

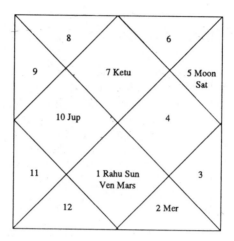

CONVEYANCE

If lord of ascendant is linked in some manner or other with 4th house, if its lord and Moon and 4th house etc. are all strong, well aspected by benefics, the native takes active part in politics, is popular with the public and is a well wisher and leader of masses.

If lords of 4th house and 11th house and Venus significator for conveyance are well posited, aspected or conjoined, the native gets comforts of conveyance. Mars, Venus, Sun and Jupiter in 4th or 11th house give the person conveyance.

Example: In example no. 2 as mentioned earlier, 4th lord Mars is in 11th house of gain and significator Venus is in 3rd aspected by Jupiter and conjoined with benefic planets. The native enjoyed good conveyance since 1964 by the grace of Lord Shiva.

CHILDREN

In this case the horoscopes of husband and wife are both to be analysed. 5th house is house of children and should be studied for all problems relating to children. On Bhavat Bhavam principle 5th to 5th is 9th house, which should also be analysed. Jupiter is significator for sons. If all of these factors are weak and afflicted in the horoscope one is denied a son. Being a sensitive issue, this is being discussed in detail.

Example: In the horoscope, provided, study carefully the application of the above rule. In the horosocope, 5th house lord Saturn is in 11th house aspecting its own sign in conjunction with Moon. 5th house too is aspected by Ketu from Lagna. 9th house lord Mercury is in dush thansa 8th house aspected by Saturn whereas Saturn is aspected by Rahu. On top of it all, significator for Son Jupiter is in debilitated sign. So the lady has been denied any male issue. Jupiter aspects 9th house lord Mercury. The aspect of Moon on 5th house is responsible for three daughters born to the lady.

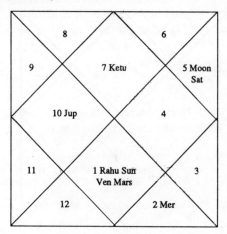

In this chart, Saturn is yogkarka but aspected by Rahu and conjoined by female planet Moon. The denial of son is due to Saturn and Jupiter. Moon, Mercury and Rahu are Vargottarna in Navamsa chart.

Hope for Sons

When Jupiter will enter Gemini in 9th house and aspect 5th house, and trine aspect on Moon, Saturn will bless the native with a son. Moreover, 9th lord in 8th house is aspected by Jupiter alongwith transitting Saturn in 3rd house. This is an apt period for begetting a son.

Like 5th, 9th house determine the number of sons the native is likely to have. If 9th house lord is strong and aspected by even a moderately strong Jupiter, one is sure to have a son even if 5th lord and 5th house are totally weak. Author of *Deva Keralam* has also confirmed this in his sloka:

"Bhagyadhip Dasa Kale Bhagya Vridhi Sutotsavah".

This means that during dasa of 9th house lord, there is increase in one's fortune and one gets a son.

Malefics in 5th House

Natural malefics such as Sun, Mars and Saturn become weak by occupying 5th house. In such cases, traits of houses over which these malefic planets have lordship, suffer. Hence, natural malefic planet having lordship of good houses but posited in 5th house requires the aspect or influence of benefic planets in order to give good effects over which they have lordship. If they do not have good aspect or influence, they do not yield good results.

Acquisition of Children

Happy is the couple blessed with children, early or late in life. A few combinations for begetting children are given below:

1. Mercury in 9th house will bless with one son only.

2. Saturn in 5th in Cancer will give many children.

3. Jupiter in Moon sign identical with 5th house gives many daughters.

4. Mars and Mercury in Cancer in 5th house will not give many children.

5. When a benefic in 11th house, and Moon and Venus occupy 5th house, first issue will be female.

6. When Moon, Mars and Venus are posited in dual sign the first child will be a son.

7. If 5th lord is in 2nd or 8th house, many daughters will be born.

8. When benefics occupy 10th and 4th houses, delivery will be after great difficulty.

9. If Taurus, Aries or Cancer happen to be in 5th house and occupied by Rahu or Ketu, there will be no delay in birth of child.

10. If 5th lord is debilitated and occupies 6th, 8th or 12th house, and is conjoined with malefics, there will be one child only.

Non-Conception

Under some planetary combinations, there may not be any conception, which may lead to her barrenness.

1. If Sun and Saturn are in Lagna and 7th house, or both are in 7th house where 10th house is aspected by Jupiter, there will be no conception.

2. If Saturn or 6th lord occupies 6th house, and Moon is in 7th house.

3. Mars and Saturn is in 6th in Watery sign.

4. If 7th house is owned by malefic as well as aspected by malefics.

5. Rahu and Sun in 7th give birth to dead children.

6. Sun in 5th and hemmed by malefics and if Saturn and Mars are in depression, the native will be childless.

7. If Taurus is Lagna and Venus is alone in 5th no children.

8. If 5th and Lagna lord are weak and if malefic is in 5th.

9. If Lagna lord and Rahu are joined and if 5th lord and Mars are conjoined.

10. Also if Jupiter is in 5th, and 9th occupied by malefics, there will be no issue to the lady.

Abortions

1. If Mars joins Jupiter and Venus in 8th, there will be many abortions.

2. If Mars occupies 8th and has aspect of Saturn, there will be an abortion.

3. If lord of Navamsa is occupied by owners of 7th, 9th and 5th houses or by malefic amsas or is conjoined with malefics.

4. If Jupiter or Venus is in 8th, dead children or abortions are indicated.

5. If 5th lord occupies malefic amsa, depression sign or is eclipsed or aspected by malefics, loss of children is there.

6. If 5th lord is occupied by owner of amsa in which 12th lord is posited, loss of children.

7. If 5th house is occupied or aspected by malefics.

8. When 5th house is occupied by benefics is in exaltation, result is loss of children.

Family Extinction

There are certain yogas in birth chart which cause destruction of family. Such yogas are enumerated below:

1. If Mercury and Lagna lord occupy any kendra except Lagna.

2. If malefics are posited in 12th, 5th and 8th houses.

3. If Moon and Jupiter are in Lagna and Saturn or Mars in 7th house.

4. If all the malefics are in 4th, destruction of family is assured.

5. If malefics occupy Ascendant, 12th, 5th and 8th or if Moon is in 5th and malefics in 8th, Lagna and 12th houses.

6. If Mercury and Venus are in 7th or 12th house, malefics in 4th, Jupiter in 5th.

7. If malefics occupy 8th house from Moon.

8. If all malefics are in 5th house, family extinction is the result.

9. If Venus is in 7th, Moon in 10th and malefics in 4th.

10. If Mars in Lagna, Saturn in 8th, Sun in 5th.

Illegitimate Children

These facts, when found in a horoscope, should not be divulged to the party for obvious reasons.

The yogas indicating illegitimate children are as below:

1. If lords of 6th and 9th are associated with malefics.

2. If lord of 2nd, 3rd, 5th and 6th all are posited in Ascendant.

3. If Rahu and Mars in Lagna, Moon and Sun in 7th, father will be of a low caste.

4. If Moon and Sun are in one house not aspected by Jupiter.

5. If lords of 1st, 4th, 6th and 9th all are conjoined in one house.

However there are certain exceptions to the above yogas, which have been detailed in author's famous book, *Saturn—a friend or a foe,* and can be referred to for further study.

Adoption of Child

At times when native is not blessed with a child, the adoption of child becomes a necessity in most cases for various reasons. Such yogas are found in the birth chart. Such yogas are:

1. If Moon and Mars conjoin in 4th house adoption of child can be predicted.

2. In case of family extinction yogas, the native will adopt a child.

3. If Moon is in 5th, either in Rasi or Navamsa of Saturn and is associated with a planet other than Saturn, the native will have a son by adoption.

4. If 9th house is afflicted by Saturn, Mandi and Lagna lord, is badly disposed to 9th house or its lord.

5. When Moon aspects Mandi in association with Saturn, one will adopt a child.

VIRILITY OR IMPOTENCE OF HUSBAND

In many cases, while studying the chart of a woman, the birth of child is predicted but the poor lady is denied this fruit. The in-laws and society declare the lady to be barren and what not. Do you think that it is only lady who has to be blamed for this misfortune? It is better to check and make a close study of the man's birth chart which will reveal that he has no virile power and may be impotent.

In this case Astrology can help such couples and direct them to a doctor and save them from troubles, disappointments, divorce, separations etc

The following are such yogas which denote loss of virile power or impotence of husband.

1. If Lagna is placed in odd sign and aspected by Mars posited in even sign.

2. If Moon is in even sign and Mercury in odd sign and both are aspected by Mars.

3. If Venus, Moon, and Lagna occupy Navamsa of odd sign.

4. When Venus and Saturn occupy 10th house.

5. When Saturn is 6th or 8th from Venus.

6. If Saturn and Venus are in 8th without any benefic aspect.

7. If Saturn is posited in 12th house in Aries.

8. If Rahu, Venus or Saturn are in exaltation, Sun in Cancer, Moon in Aries, the person is devoid of virile strength.

9. If Moon is in Lagna and Jupiter and Saturn in 5th house.

10. If Virgo is Ascendant aspected by Saturn, Mercury and Venus occupying sign of Saturn, it indicates loss of virile power.

11. Add together the figures and latitude of Jupiter, Moon and Mars in the case of Female Horoscopes. If the result denotes an even rasi and even amsa, the strength of fecundity in the female for producing offsprings is assured. If it is mixed, viz. rasi male or amsa female or vice versa, there will be children after great efforts.

12. If sum total of latitudes of Sun, Venus and Jupiter signify odd rasi and an odd navamsa, it denotes that the virility in male to produce child is very strong, and in case one of the two rasis and navamsa is even, mixed results are indicated.

13. Subtract five times the figures for the Sun from five times the figures for the Moon. If tithi represented by the result is an auspicious one in the bright half of the month, progeny is assured. (Tithis 4th, 6th, 8th, 9th, 12th and 14th all are inauspicious).

TRAVELS

There is always a charm and thrill in travels. Sometimes travelling is for some definite purpose or for the sake of pleasure and recreations. So there is much curiosity about travel prospects in the mind of people.

But astrologically, we have to see whether or not such a travel is destined. Will such travel be useful, profitable or not? Starting in rashness and ending in a crash should not be the fate of such travels. In order to check, we provide a few guidelines.

In a birth chart 3rd house denotes short journeys whereas 9th house denotes foreign travels.

The persons whose Ascendant falls in Aries, Cancer, Libra and Capricorn like to travel. Such natives like some activity of any sort all the while and they cannot afford to be idle. These signs are cardinal signs or movable signs. Persons with fixed signs such as Leo, Scorpio, Taurus and Aquarius seldom feel any inclination to move from one place to another. These signs are of fixed nature. But when such persons decide to go out, they need a well planned, organised programme with all the arrangements made in advance. Not certainly either way can be indicated in respect of persons wth Gemini, Virgo, Sagittarius and Pisces Ascendants (Mutable signs), but usually, they prove to be good companions when on journey.

Elements and Qualities

Remember this table by heart, it will facilitate you to analyse.

	Fire	*Water*	*Air*	*Earth*
Cardinal (Movable)	Aries	Cancer	Libra	Capricorn
Fixed	Leo	Scorpio	Aquarius	Taurus
Mutable (common)	Sagittarius	Pisces	Gemini	Virgo

Role of Planets

Saturn is planet of limitations and restrictions, has usually aversion to travel. ·Saturnian persons undertake journey when it is absolutely necessary, not otherwise.

Moon is responsible for the eagerness to move. Persons in whose chart Moon is in watery signs are always ready to travels.

Sun, planet of vitality, and Jupiter of expansion encourage the native to go on journeys for some specific purpose such as profession, service and some religious work.

Venus, planet of love and beauty always brings about luxury and pleasure trips.

Mars, the planet of heat and energy always induces a man to take up adventurous journeys regardless of future consequences.

Mercury does not indicate anything special in this respect.

When to Travel

Leaving aside the daily journeys, an auspicious time has to be chosen when one feels inclined to go on a long voyage, either by rail, road or by air for some specific mission. We only wish it to be a successful and safe trip.

In a horoscope 6th, 8th and 12th houses are inauspicious whereas 1st, 3rd, 5th, 7th, 9th, 10th and 11th are auspicious and of vital importance. Transit of planets in these houses is regarded as auspicious to travel. For long travels, dasa and bhuktis are also to be considered important.

For short journeys, the auspicious transit of Moon in 1st, 4th, 5th, 7th, 9th, 10th and 11th houses is considered to be sufficient. Such journeys always remain comfortable and fulfil the purpose of travel.

For long journeys, the transit of slow moving planets in these~ houses is very important. It would be helpful to consult some experienced astrologer on such occasions.

Air Journey

For travel by air, airy sign, Gemini, Libra and especially Aquarius are essentially be taken into consideration. Any affliction to these signs by planets always create some air disaster.

A common question posed is "Will I go abroad?" or "Any foreign travel for me?" which is analysed as under:

1. Houses 1st, 3rd, 9th and 12th are to be judged alongwith their lords.

2. If 12th house lord is retrograde or aspected by malefics, one cannot go to a foreign country. If 12th lord is direct and is connected with 3rd, 9th or 12th house in any way, one will go abroad.

3. Intimate links between 1st, 2nd, 7th and 11th houses and links with Rahu or Saturn denote air travel (3, 7, 11 houses are airy houses).

4. Lords of 1st, Moon and Ascendant are the significators, 9th and its lord are the significator of the voyage.

5. When the lords of 1st and 9th change place or aspect with each other, or with Moon or the luminaries in 11th or strong in 1st or 9th house or Rahu is in 9th, there are signs of prosperous voyages.

6. If lords of 1st and 9th or Moon is oriented with respect to Sun, or swift or in movable signs, the voyage will be quick, but slower if accidental, slow, or in fixed signs.

7. If lord of Lagna is retrograde or if Moon applies to retrograde planet, no good will come of the undertaking and the traveller will turn back before he reaches his destination.

8. If Lagna lord or Moon is in 6th, 8th or 12th, the native will suffer much sickness, and the same if in conjunction with evil aspects or malefics.

9. If luminaries are afflicted, and the Moon or Lagna lord is near

violent fixed stars or a malefic or violent star ascending, there
will be a danger of untimely death.

10. If Saturn afflicts significators, it denotes sickness and loss, but
     if the afflicting planet is Mars, it denotes battles, piracy, fire,
     lightning etc.

11. If Lagna lord, 9th lord and Moon are in conjunction with each
     other or with the Ascendant or in evil aspect either with each
     other or with the malefics, the journey will be inauspicious.

12. The 9th house, its lord, Sun or Moon, being afflicted denotes
     sickness and disaster.

Will Aeroplanes Reach Safely?

This is a very vital question to be checked for any mishap, hijacking,
engine trouble, explosion, sabotage and fire accident caused to the
aeroplane. Lords of 1st, 8th and of Moon sign and Moon answer this
question.

1. If all the four planets are being aspected by benefic, the plane
    will reach safely at the place of destination.

2. If all the four planets are being ill aspected or afflicted, the
    plane will not reach safely and may meet with any accident
    during the journey.

3. If 10th lord is posited in 8th or 12th house, the plane will be
    hijacked or taken to some other place or direction.

4. If 10th and 6th house lords are posited in 3rd, there will be
    some trouble en route.

5. If 4th lord is Saturn aspected by Moon or in 8th house there
    will be some theft of the baggage in the plane.

TESTIMONY: To check the authenticity of the above rules, take the
chart on 10th/11th September 1976 at Palam Delhi Airport, when Air
India flight No. 111 took off at 1.25 a.m. by which the daughter of the
author left for New York and reached there safely.

The 1st rule is to be judged, lord of Ascendant is Gemini (Airy sign) where lord is Mercury, 8th house lord is Saturn, Moon sign lord is Jupiter and Moon. These four factors are to be analysed.

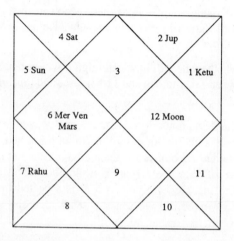

Moon is 2nd house lord, this house is beneficial. Mercury is under sextile aspect of Saturn whereas Jupiter fully aspects Mercury and in sextile to Saturn. Jupiter too has sextile aspect on Moon. Moon is being aspected by Lagna lord. Jupiter is under sextile aspect of Moon.

So all the four factors are aspected in a benefic way resulting in the safe landing of the aeroplane at New York. The journey was most comfortable.

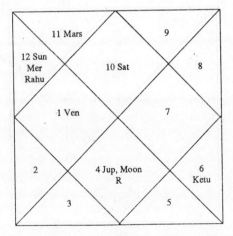

2. A lady born on 18/19th March, 1932 at 5 a.m. at Longitude 24.26°E and Latitude 31.8°N corresponding to 7th Chetra Bikrami Sanvat 1990.

Capricorn is rising. Jupiter is exalted, Moon in own sign in 7th house. Lagna lord Saturn in own sign in Lagna. Ketu is in Mootrikona rasi. Jupiter is retrograde at birth.

To check whether she will have a foreign travel or not, we have to check links between 1st, 2nd, 7th and 11th houses and link with Rahu or Saturn as enumerated above.

Lagna lord and 2nd house lord is Saturn, and posited in own signs, both houses, are linked. 7th house lord in 7th with 3rd and 12th house lord Jupiter exalted in 7th both are aspecting Lagna. Jupiter is aspecting 11th house. Lord of 11th house Mars is in 2nd house. So all the four houses are linked together. 7th and its lord is aspected by Rahu and Saturn itself is involved. So we can say safely that she will have a foreign travel by air.

As stated earlier dasa and bhukti should also be checked. The lady (wife of author) left for Singapore on 9/10th July 1983 at 2.45 a.m. from Delhi when she was running Rahu Mahadasa and Rahu Bhukti.

3. Again on 29th/30th July 1988 at 2.35 a.m. from Delhi she left for New York during Rahu Mahadasa and Saturn antra which remain up to 9 April 1990.

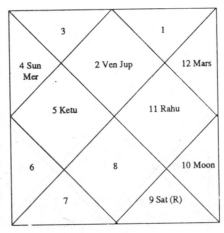

TESTIMONY: The horoscope of the moment when the plane left Delhi is shown. She had to change planes at Frankfurt to reach New York. This chart is of 29th/30th July 1988 at 2.35 a.m. at Delhi.

Lagna lord is in Lagna with 8th and 11th house lord Jupiter. 10th lord Saturn in 8th house.

Under rule 3 for aeroplanes, the plane went in another direction.

It so happened that the flight for New York from Frankfurt was cancelled. After six hours of ordeal, another flight took off for New York via Washington, so she had to take the flight through another direction. So this dictum is confirmed. The plane reached New York at 3 a.m. next day and she had to take a flight for Rochester at 4.10 p.m. To stay for 12 hours was a problem for her. So she went to New Jersy to visit relations and then reached her final destination. Her baggage was misplaced during changeovers but finally was delivered to her after 2 days by the Airlines.

Again check rule 5 which clearly indicates loss of baggage etc. Moon sign lord Saturn is retrograde and in the 8th house causes worries. 4th house is posited with Ketu causing family worries to all there and at Delhi. How correct is this science?

Note: She was advised to go on 28th/29th July 1988, which she refused due to her preoccupations and hence suffered the ordeal.

SERVICE OR BUSINESS

Nowadays, with the passage of time and all round development there are so many professions that it is difficult to pinpoint a specific career, however the nature of employment or profession of a native can be described. There are various professions multifarious in nature, and so many causes far beyond the individual's control or inclination which force one to follow a line or enter into a service for which one has neither taste nor aptitude. Moreover, to analyse fully the several professions and to bring them under separate heads, we should know the nature of planets fully and also of the various degrees of Zodiac in terms of the professions.

The environment, education, and mental tendencies of a native sometimes vary and shape the nature of vocation.

In service, one is not independent, his fate is tied with someone else or authority. He receives a fixed amount of salary on the fixed day. The businessman is free to decide his fortune at his own sweet will, he can earn thousands of rupees in the twinkling of an eye and may lose lakhs also.

On this basis, we analyse the problem astrologically.

In a horoscope, 2nd, 11th, 5th, 9th houses and planets therein are the indicators of fluctuating and abounding money gains. Persons having sound planetary positions in these houses should go in for business. Efficiency, luck, daring, inventive methods, proper employment of persons and partners are some of the additional meritorious points which are required to be considered for business.

Business

A planet or a group of planets which has particular bearings on assorted business lines is required for reckoning with first. Besides, a businessman must have inborn and insatiable thirst for earning money. In technical terms, it is called "acquisitiveness" or greedy tendencies. Planets in 2nd or 11th house indicate such trends, Taurus, Virgo, and Capricorn which are earthy signs hunger for money and unlimited possession.

The Sun represents power, authority and power of self-expression and assertion. Mars gives courage or at times encourages unthoughtful actions and adventures. Venus stands for finance and luck. Mercury for intelligence, Jupiter indicates steady luck and prosperous position, Saturn as an efficient organiser denotes insight and foresight.

Refer to the horoscope. The native is a Multi-millionaire. Analyse yourself.

Service

Service persons must possess a loyal and faithful character. Fiery signs Aries, Leo and Sagittarius indicate loyalty and devotion. They tend to make the individuals do their job sincerely and faithfully to the expectation and satisfaction of their officers or Government, or nation. Planets in 10th house do indicate tendencies of the servants. Scorpions are good for secret service, Saturn gives judicial tendencies if aspected by Jupiter, and renders political acumen and a crafty nature.

Sun, Mars if afflicted, denounce power and authority ruthlessly regardless of consequences. However, arrogance and stubborn attitude towards authority are bad qualities for a servant. Inauspicious aspects between Sun and Saturn restrict power and authority and are not considered good. Saturn brings coldness and indifference and creates undue consciousness of rights. Moon, Mars if afflicted, prompt people to act temperamentally. All these qualities are not good for servicemen.

Part-time Job

Some professionals, doctors and engineers etc. in addition to their normal service, find luck in private practice, either officially or unofficially. At times, their extra income exceeds their normal monthly salaries.

In such a person's horoscope, 2nd house and planets therein alongwith aspects are important, which indicate extra income, which can be checked alongwith dasa, bhukti etc.

Rules

To find out one's profession, our texts have laid down that:

1. Planets posited in 10th house and lord of 10th house should be checked.

2. The navamsa sign occupied by them.

3. The lords of navamsa sign in which occupants of 10th house and 10th lords are posited.

4. Judge the profession signified by the lords of navamsa signs occupied by occupant of 10th house and 10th house lord.

In Jataka Parijat it is laid down that for checking the profession:

Count from Lagna or Moon sign and note which planet occupies the 10th. Or find out 10th lords from Lagna, Sun and Moon (Sudarshan). Judge the strongest of the lords. Note in which navamsa sign the strongest of the lords of 10th house is counted from 'Sudarshan', then find out who rules the navamsa sign. This lord is indicator of profession.

5. A planet highly dominant or strong in birth chart will indicate profession.

6. If there are benefic aspects between Mercury and Jupiter, Mercury and Mars, Mercury and Venus and Mars and Venus, the native should choose an intellectual job.

Example: Check the horoscope. Refer to Rule 4, 5 and 6 supra on the chart.

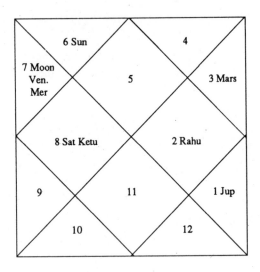

(i)   10th from Sun is Mars
      10th from Moon is Moon sign Cancer,
      10th from Lagna is Rahu;

(ii) Strongest planets in the chart are Mars and Jupiter;

(iii) Mercury, Venus and Moon have aspect of Jupiter. Mars has sextile aspect over Moon, Venus and Mercury, all aspects are benefic.

Mars, Jupiter indicate Civil Engineer and 10th house Taurus denotes water; a class 1 officer in Irrigation Department is an Engineer.

He worked on Astrology (Jupiter) and is author of fourteen books on occult sciences.

Planets

Finally, we provide what profession each planet and sign indicates and when we blend them as above, we are able to in most cases.

1. *Sun:* It rules over kings, persons in power and authority. Government favours, royal appointments like IAS, magistrates, medical persons, administrative posts, auditing and accountancy, etc.

2. *Moon:* Moon rules over ladies, travellers, sailors, nurses, midwives, textiles, dairy products, navy, hotels, liquids, ladies garments, irrigation and women's welfare.

3. *Mars:* Mars indicates civil engineering, soldier, army, hunting, circus, lawyers, ambassadors, lands, property dealers, spying and wicked company. Armed service, electrical engineers, butchers, atomic energy, postal services, contractor, etc.

4. *Mercury:* Mercury denotes salesmanship, school teachers, orators, accountants, poets, editors, printers, publishers, clerical service, auditing, insurance agents, postal departments and authors.

5. *Venus:* Indicates artistic, musical and pleasurable pursuits, jewellers, hotels, cabaret houses, restaurants, horse races, milk, perfumes, ladies' articles, pictures, flowers, dealing with the fair sex, cookery, medicine, etc.

6. *Jupiter:* Indicates commerce, trade, favours from people and Government, service, law, religious institutions and money-lending. Astrology, revenue, irrigation department, judges, scholars, authors, political career, income-tax department, etc.

7. *Saturn:* Denotes farming, medical services, insurance, land, property, mines, petrol, kerosene oil, iron and steel, panchayats, community development works, labour, spirituality, analytical or research work, occult subjects, leather, astronomy, sanyas. All works pertaining to underground, canals, sewerage, mines etc.

8. *Rahu:* Rahu indicates radio, T.V., space travel, circus, aviation, spiritual healings, etc.

9. *Ketu:* Ketu refers to foreign trade, secret enemies, clairvoyance, mesmerism and palmistry.

Signs

1. *Aries*: Professions are connected with army, defence department, surgeons, police, chemists, lawyers, iron and steel, machines, factories, industries, sports goods, etc.

2. *Taurus*: Denotes trade in luxury goods, cosmetics, scents, jewels, gems, etc. Connected with finance, music, pleasure resorts, cinema, actors, film producers, agriculture, etc. Transport, irrigation, income-tax departments, ladies clubs and schools, fashion and beauty parlours, dealers in ladies garments and beauty items.

3. *Gemini*: The professions are connected with brokers, businessmen, advocates, secretaries, journalists, travelling agents and jobs connected with them.

4. *Cancer*: Articles derived from water, like pearls, conch, sailors in navy, submarines, shipping department, import or export and travels. Good caterer, restaurant managers, contractors, orators, good job in irrigation department. Development of Vedic and sacred texts.

5. *Leo*: High position in government, managers of big concerns, corporations, directors, positions of power and authorities in these areas, also captains, sales managers, etc.

6. *Virgo*: Shows brokers, accountants, lawyers, journalists, engineers, surgeons, works connected with liquids, etc.

7. *Libra*: Government servants and officers, lawyers, chemists, sales of liquid items, electrical engineers, transport, navy, painters, etc. Dealers in ladies articles, amusements, writers, musicians, playback singers, actors, architects and good salesmen.

8. *Scorpio*: Indicates chemistry, medicine, insurance, maternity department, surgeon, chemists, research work, C.I.D. detectives, iron and steel work, military and navy department, etc.

9. *Sagittarius*: Teachers, professors, priests, public speakers, politicians, bank employees, professions related to religion and educational institutions. Editing and publishing. Company law, civil engineering, contractors, foreign assignments, etc.

10. *Capricorn*: Business dealing with kerosene oil, petrol, land, animal, irrigation departments, contractors, agriculture, engineers, cement

manufacturing, lawyers, brick kiln owners, scientific instruments, clubs, societies, long term contracts, mines and land products. Chemical, leather and hides, etc.

11. *Aquarius*: Scientists, good executives, positions in large offices or concerns, lecturers, astrologers, legal, finance, or education advisors, mine contractors or dealers in shipping and export.

12. *Pisces*: Bankers, accountants, music and opera houses, cinema, occult sciences, actors, good businessmen, liaison officers, managing directors, or chairmen, navy, shipping corporations, etc. Dealers in drinks, oils, beverages, cosmetics, chemicals, medical and education departments, etc.

PLANETS AND POLITICS

The Zodiac has been divided into three groups, Fixed, Cardinal (movable) and Common. Leo, Taurus, Scorpio and Aquarius fall in fixed groups, these persons are rightly called conservatives and are fixed in outlook. If these signs and lords are afflicted they become stupid, tyrannical, or dictatorial. The second group of Gemini, Virgo, Sagittarius and Pisces are Cardinal or movable signs—practical, adaptable and flexible. They lack in confidence and are mostly capable of shouldering heavy responsibilities, are highly emotional and touchy.

The third group is of common signs. Aries, Capricorn, especially Cancer and Libra are positive in action, have pushful drive, are dominating, energetic and enthusiastic. These people move by emotions and feelings. They have an inborn tendency to endure and sacrifice and stick to certain ideas and ideals. Though they move with masses yet they guide and control them with determination, courage and foresight. They have a dynamic outlook. Either Librans or Cancerian type of leaders have so far been able to lead the countries to the heights of glory and helped the masses to free them from slavery and dependence.

Popularity: 4th house in a birth chart indicates masses. Moon is said to be the planet of masses or people at large. Hence it is essential that 4th house, its lord, significator Moon and Cancer sign in a birth chart be strong and aspected by benefics to enable one to become popular in public. Other signs are Venus and Libra. So both these planets, their signs Libra and Cancer must be strong, both by sign and house wise in the chart of a politician.

Politics

The following combinations are responsible for a person to be in politics

1. Sun, a planet of power and authority and royalty, indicates favour from government and superiors. So Sun must be strong, well placed and well aspected particularly from Jupiter.

2. Mars indicating push, zeal, forwardness must be strong.

3. 4th house indicates the public. So 4th house should contain benefic aspects and planets and its lord should be strong and well placed, then only can one get favour and support from public.

4. Jupiter and Mercury be favourable to be a good orator and Mars must be auspicious to enable him to carry the masses with him.

5. Jatak Parijat contains that if Sun, Mercury and Saturn are conjoined, one becomes a minister.

6. Sun, Moon, Mercury, Jupiter and Venus (Panchayat of Planets) conjoined in a house and well aspected makes one a minister.

7. Jupiter in 9th house, aspects of Mars is beneficial.

8. Three planets in own signs makes one a minister. He or she may be tactful, diplomatic and clever or cunning and a hypocrite.

9. If lord of 5th is in 4th, one will be a minister in youth and an honest one. It is so said in Sanketa Nidhi.

10. Sun in 6th makes one a minister, so says Horasara. So also Jupiter in 6th or Venus in 5th or 10th gives the person the rank of a minister.

11. When all benefics are in 3rd, 6th, 10th or 11th and malefics in Lagna or 10th house, one becomes a chief minister.

12. Jatak Desmarya says that benefics in 6th, 7th, 8th from Moon sign, makes one a minister. Also if 10th lord is in exalted sign.

13. Phaldeepika stipulates that Mercury makes one a good orator and politician. 5th house and Jupiter alongwith Sun and Mars should be checked.

To Win Election

In the present politically dominated world, everyone is anxious to hold a political post and wants to adopt politics as a career. Astrology guides in such cases.

During election many apply for tickets to win but only a few get tickets. One person has to win against many candidates for one seat.

Jupiter plays a significant role. Good position of Jupiter in a natal chart is a must. Alongwith transit of Jupiter, it should be favourable, 10th house and Saturn too play a good part in transit. So unless Jupiter, Saturn and Mars are not favourable in transit and 10th house or its lords are not powerful, success is not possible. Check the chart with Ascendant and 10th house as Ascendant also.

The following combinations may be checked for victory in an election.

1. Jupiter must transit kendra or trikona in the 10th house or its lord.

2. When Lagna lord or yogkarka is associated with 10th house or its lord.

3. When Saturn or Mars transits 6th house or aspects 6th house during transit, even when Saturn is nearing 3rd, 6th or 11th house.

4. When lords of 1st, 5th, 9th and 10th houses are interconnected.

5. When Jupiter transits 2nd, 5th, 10th or 11th from 10th house or its lord, or from the natal position or its natal sign.

Use of Sudarshan Chakra must be made and followed. 10th house from Lagna, Sun and Moon and 7th house as additional house should be considered and checked. Even if three of the five points mentioned above are secured in the horoscope, the chances of victory are quite good but more than three points assure victory.

PLANETS AND SPIRITUALITY

Jupiter is karka or significator for spiritual illumination, Mercury is karka for intellect, worldly knowledge, and learning. Moon indicates mind and heart. For spiritual attainment, control of mind and heart is essential since mind is the cause of ego, attachment, bondage and slavery to passions and desires. Jupiter's association, aspect etc., with Moon brings discipline of mind and control of emotions and opens the mysterious window in the secret chamber of the heart and brings about consciousness of God.

Saturn, a great friend of a native indicates the way for the spiritual realisation through renunciations. Saturn can be called lord of purgation, disillusionment, remuneration etc. Saturn is the chastener, the subduer and awakener of the dormant divinity within.

So Jupiter plays an important part alongwith other planets for spiritual attainment, enlightenment and realisation.

Horoscope of Sri Satya Sai Baba

Sri Satya Sai Baba was born on 23rd November 1926 at Puttaparti, a tiny village in Andhra Pradesh, at a time when the Sun just rose above the horizon. The birth chart and position of planets are shown.

The Lagna is Libra, Venus the lord has bestowed on Baba sweetness and godliness. Aspected by Mars, indicates a radiant and fascinating personality. The conjunction of Sun, Mercury, Venus and Saturn in 2nd house has made him slight and short, with dark eyes, soft and luminous and bright face with inner tranquillity and bliss. Mars' position in the chart has made him a leader and is forming Ruchka yaga and such persons are courageous, bold, well-versed in ancient lores, famous like a king. Mars in nakshatra of Venus and aspecting Lagna, also 2nd lord have given him a melodious voice.

It is said in old treatises that if Saturn or Lagna lord aspect the sign occupied by Moon, a tapasvi, a man of great asceticism is born, here this combination is found. Mercury, lord of 9th is in Scorpio. Not only Saturn, a yogkarka planet but even Venus, a Lagna lord conjoining Mercury with Atma karka planet Sun, Vidya Karka Mercury, Kavya Karka Venus in Scorpio make Babaji a native of dynamic personality.

The grouping of these planets has given rise to member of Rajyogas like Lakshmi yoga, Adhiyoga, Buddha Aditya yoga which confer on him comforts, wealth, eminence and power.

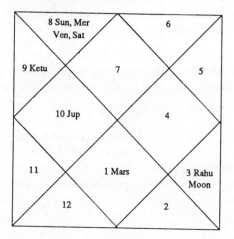

When lord of sign in which the lord of house occupied by the ascendant lord is posited in a kendra or own rasi Parajtha yoga is formed. In this chart, Mars fulfils this condition. This yoga indicates that one holds religious authority over people, receives homage from kings and rulers, possesses elephants, adheres to ancient wisdom and traditions, attains eminence and is humanitarian and generous. All these characteristics are found in Sai Baba.

5th house stands for sidhi or psychic powers, its lord Saturn yog karka planet is a clearcut symbol of this and is posited in 2nd house, 10th from 5th bringing supernatural powers. Saturn with Mercury 9th lord, with Lagna lord Venus, with Sun the atma karka planet and with 11th house lord of gains, bestows miraculous powers. The whole yoga is in the house of speech or preaching.

Jupiter though debilitated in Capricorn is in Bhava Sandhi, comes to 5th house and is therefore inherently associated with 1st, 5th and 9th houses of spirituality. All the four planets in 2nd house are in nakshatras of Saturn, a sidhi-giver planet. The powers of miracle are desired from Mars aspecting Lagna as well as 2nd house.

Wealth for a yogi is spiritual treasure, 2nd house indicates wealth and its lord Mars has connection with Lagna, lord of the masses. Saturn denotes that the native utilises his wealth of spirituality with the masses. Yogkarka Saturn is connected with Lagna lord and Mars, lord of 10th from 10th denotes untiring zeal and position of success.

So the horoscope of Sri Sai Baba indicates that he is not only a man of miracles but a man of self-enlightenment blessed with rich spiritual power and realisation, also with psychic and spiritual affluence.

TRANSFERS

Transfer of a government servant or private employee affects the person financially, mentally and physically. Whether minor or a major change, it disturbs one's, normal working; these transfers sometimes are undesirable but in some cases profitable. In yet others, they are inevitable.

Houses

The houses involved are 4th, 7th, 10th and Ascendant. If 10th house, a house of profession or vocational activities, has any affliction with other houses it creates possibilities of transfer and shift. The ascendant or Lagna denotes personality and environments. 4th house denotes family's welfare and domestic life. 7th house comes directly in aspect with Lagna or in square aspect with 10th house and 4th. So all kendra houses are connected with transfer.

When 4th house is afflicted, the transfer may cause separation from family.

Zodiacal Signs

Aries, Libra, Cancer and Capricorn being movable are signs prone to transfers. Taurus, Leo, Scorpio and Aquarius being fixed signs are inclined to fixity of stay, they have peculiar liking for a particular place; if transferred, may forego promotion if the place is not to their liking. No definite indications can be given to common sign Gemini, Virgo, Sagittarius and Pisces, unless planets placed in the signs are considered; they prefer transfer only on promotions.

Planets

Any affliction to radical Sun, a planet of power and authority, brings transfer or changes in the life of a servant. Affliction of Saturn causes loss of prestige, respect, status and finances. Also may cause unforeseen changes, scandals, prejudices and enquiries involving immediate transfer.

Mars creates abrupt changes, energetic activities and enthusiasm in the house where placed. Its transit in the above four houses creates possible changes against the wish and will of the individual. Persons having Mars or Sun in 10th house, or Lagna, or 4th in the birth chart should always remember that transit of Mars over these planets is mostly accompanied by transfer.

Saturn being a slow moving planet stabilises the position. It brings confinement to a place for years together.

Proceeding on Leave

Proceeding on leave is absence from duty with or without sanction, willingly or unwillingly. When Sun or Mars transits in the 4th or 7th house, one is likely to proceed on leave by force or willingly.

Example: The native with Leo Lagna had fixity of stay, liking a particular place for posting and during 27 years of service had only 5 transfers and that too mostly on promotions but Saturn being in 4th house of family kept him separated from family.

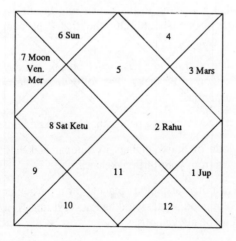

LUCK IN SPECULATIONS

Speculation includes lotteries, gambling, stock and share, racing. All points except racing fall under one heading.

Lotteries gambling and stock share—out of the three, the cheapest is lottery. With one ticket of small amount, you aspire for lakhs of rupees in a single day. In order to control illicit gambling, various state government have started and regularised gambling in a decent way legally.

Many people want to become "Get Rich Quick". Lots of people with soaring hopes buy the tickets but only a few are lucky to get the prize. But in speculative gains special luck is required which differs from man to man and depends on the individual horoscopes.

Rules: 5th, 2nd and 11th houses, their lords and planets posited therein are required to be judged very carefully to assess special luck in a lottery or speculative gain. 5th house stands for speculation, also is of "Purva Karma" or "Prarabdha", or "Sanchit", whereas 11th house is house of gain and 2nd house stands for inflow of money and wealth. Unless these houses are posited or their lords are properly placed and aspected by benefics, no man should be considered lucky to gain through lotteries, gambling and stock and shares, including racing.

When to Purchase Tickets

If one is sure that according to the above rule he/she is sufficiently fortunate or lucky, one should buy the ticket or coupon on the auspicious day.

Check the date of draw, one has to pick up a proper day or an event to purchase a coupon to be lucky. The following three rules may be considered as auspicious.

1.   Transitting Moon must be in 5th, 11th or 2nd house.

2.   The Moon or major planets in Sampat Nakshatra, viz. 2nd nakshatra from your birth nakshatra.

3.   Moon or other auspicious planets for a particular Ascendant must form good aspect with the Paras Fortuna, if it is properly placed in the above houses.

Horse Racing

Some people have fascination for this royal sport either as a game or for getting rich quickly.

First of all, he/she must confirm from a competent astrologer whether one has luck in gambling and racing. Houses in birth chart responsible for indicating the success are mainly 11, 5, 2, 9 and 10. Even in daily transactions, businessmen and professionals will mainly witness that transit of planets including Moon always brings unusual profits and gains. Unless these houses or their lords have inherent strength, no person should consider himself lucky or fortunate in speculative activities. He should check that major planets or at least the Moon are transitting in those houses, especially in 11th or 5th houses. Otherwise, whatever may be the prospective card, hints, tips and suggestions, one should not indulge in such fluctuating games.

When one is sure of success on a particular day on the above basis then the question of particular choice of horse in a particular race or event arises.

NUMBERS

In numbers and according to Hebraic, the following numbers have been assigned to various planets.

Sun	Morning	1,	Afternoon	4
Moon	"	7,	"	2
Jupiter		3		
Venus		6		
Mercury		5		
Saturn		8		
Mars		9		

Draw a chart indicating time of race, place and date. The planets on the Ascendant, 10th and 5th, 7th and 9th houses are the real indicators of winners as first, second, third etc.

7

HOW TO CONTROL MISFORTUNES IN ONE'S LIFE

There are various methods to control the calamities of life. Our Maharishis have shown us the way in this materialistic world by which we can fulfil our desires and seek worldly comforts. This way is through Mantra, Tantra and Yantra which termed *Tantrik Remedies*.

To control or minimise the planetary malefic effects, there are ways of propitiations, which appease or conciliate and in Hindi is used as *Upaye* for the planets which are weak, malefic by virtue of their position and create trouble for the native. These remedies have been suggested to ward off or minimise the evil effects of such afflicted planets.

The readers, after studying this book, will be curious to know the details, method and other conditions of remedies, which the author has elaborated in his book titled, *Complete Astro Palmistry* which can be referred to. However for the guidance of readers, we provide below the synopsis of the same.

Positions of Planets

The planets which are found weak, malefic or unfavourable by virtue of their position, create troubles for the native and it becomes quite imperative to remedy or mitigate the evil effects of such positions of the planets which can be summed up as:

1. Sun or Ketu in 5th, 7th or 8th house causes too many troubles.

2. Mars or Rahu in 2nd, 8th or 9th house causes many troubles and strifes.

3. Moon posited in 6th or 8th house becomes dangerously evil when weak and afflicted.

4. Mercury in 6th, 8th or 12th house becomes weak.

5. Jupiter and Saturn when posited in their debilitated signs make the native miserables.

6. Venus in 3rd, 6th, 8th or 12th houses becomes too weak and makes the native too feeble.

7. Benefics in 3rd, 6th houses give tremendous troubles.

There can be many other positions where they can create troubles and mischief.

These malefic effects can be minimised or mitigated if benefic aspects are on the planets.

PROPITIATIONS OF EVIL PLANETS

In order to get relief from such adverse positions and to avoid miseries, turmoils and troubles, the propitiations have to be made to obtain protection from the evil results. Such planets can be strengthened to ward off the evil results.

There are various ways to mitigate such evil effects and are known as *Remedies.*

1. Through articles, gems and colours of planets.
2. Through Tantric methods.
3. Through prayer and meditation.

Methods and Periods of Remedies

1. In Hindu Shastras, remedy should be carried out for a minimum of 40 days and maximum for 43 days continuously.

2. Remedies should be carried out between sunrise and sunset and should be started on the proper day.

3. If a planet is malefic and the native is unmarried, the remedies should be carried out at the time of marriage of the native and this will prove fruitful.

4. Remedies should be carried out by the person affected by malefic planets and not by others.

Remedies for Immediate Relief

Some immediate reliefs can be obtained from the following remedies:

1. *Sun:* Gur should be thrown in running water.

2. *Moon:* A container of milk or water should be kept near your head at night, and offered to Kikar tree in the morning.

3. *Mars:* (i) Sweets and sweet food should be offered or *Patasha* (made of Sugar) thrown into running water. Use of deer's skin is beneficial.

4. *Mercury:* A piece of copper with a hole should be thrown in running water.

5. *Jupiter:* Saffron should either be eaten or applied on naval or on tongue.

6. *Venus:* Offering of cow, jowar or milk to be made.

7. *Saturn:* Offering of mustard oil.

8. *Rahu:* Coal to be thrown in river. Offering of *radish* is also recommended.

9. *Ketu:* Part of your food should be given to a well-bred dog.

GEMS

Cosmic radiations of which the body is composed of, becomes imbalanced and so Astral Gems are used, which are to be carefully selected as they effect the human. body through their measured radiations.

The selection of gems is very difficult. Actually one should wear two stones simultaneously. One ruling planet stone should be a permanent one and the other for the malefic planet to ward off evils.

The second point is that when a planet is malefic in a chart and use of the stone of that planet is prescribed, then in author's views the hands of that planet have been strengthened by giving him an added strength or power to do more evils. What is required to be used is *Anti Dose Treatment* to the planet in order to minimise the evil results.

Dr. Oscar Brunler of USA has measured the radiations of gems and planets. Gems are used for medicinal use also. Their vibrations are continuously absorbed in the body. Care should be taken in selection of ,jewels, otherwise reverse results can be expected.

Wave Lengths of Jewels and Planets

Planet	Wave Length (-ve)	Gems of Planets	Hindi Name	Wave Length (+ve)	Nature of Gem	Colour of Gem
1. Sun	65,000	Ruby	Manak	70,000	Hot	Red
2. Moon	65,000	Pearl	Moti	70,000	Cold	White
3. Mars	85,000	Coral	Moonga	65,000	Hot	Yellow
4. Mercury	85,000	Emerald	Panna	70,000	Hot	Green
5. Jupiter	1,30,000	Topaz	Pukhraj	50,000	Cold	Blue
6. Venus	1,30,000	Diamond	Hira	80,000	Hot	Indigo
7. Saturn	65,000	Sapphire	Neelam	70,000	Too cold	Violet
8. Rahu	35,000	Hassonite	Gomed	70,000	Cold	Ultra violet
9. Ketu	35,000	Cat's eye	Lahsaniya	70,000	Too Hot	Infra Red

Traits of Gems

Gems in addition to warding off the evil effects of planets can be used for other useful purposes also. They increase the psychic powers of the native. For example, emerald increases the brain power, remedies fickle mindedness, stammering, loss of memory, etc. In such cases, when emerald is worn it will continue to vibrate incessantly the benefic powers of Mercury. Other can be used likewise.

The planets control the seven systems of the human body. There are seven Dhatus in the body, namely chyle, blood, flesh, fat, bone, marrow and semen and the seven planets that have lordship over seven Dhatus respectively are Saturn, Moon, Mercury, Jupiter, Sun, Mars and Venus.

Accordingly gems have curative powers on diseases when the planets cause the disease.

The traits of gems are only summarised for the guidance of readers. Selection of gems should be made very carefully to propitiate the planets and are worn on the correct day and on the correct finger of the right hand or working hand and with correct metal and weight.

Gems should not be removed from the body. It takes months before the action of gems becomes manifest in body but the moment it is removed, the benefic effects are disconnected and instantly lost.

Warning: The planets obviously do not help sinful persons in evil work. Such persons who indulge in bad actions, bad thoughts and bad habits are swayed by greed, hatred, and injury and when they invoke the powers of jewels to better their conditions, they invariably meet with disaster. For them it is dangerous to wear jewels of any kind, and the chances are that they will not only not receive any benefic results, but their fall is a certainty.

1. *Ruby:* A hot stone and can be used for the development of soul force, to be used in summer months. It cures peptic ulcer, fever, rheumatism, gout, etc. Its constant use may cause boils, itch and insomnia. The use of ruby should be avoided by ladies as it destroys the body lustre. To be used in gold in third or ring finger of right hand on Sunday. Manak should be of about 3 or 5 grams in weight.

2. *Pearl:* Pearl or Moti is used to remove the evil effects of Moon and it strengthens the mind force, increases good sleep and cures insomnia. It also gives good memory, cures uterine disorders, heart and eye troubles, also T.B., constipation, hysteria, pleurisy, etc. Pearl is very useful for ladies as it increases their beauty and facial lustre and will keep them ever young. Controls the rash temperament as it is a cold gem. It increases sexual strength and makes the conjugal life happy. Removes melancholy and increases fortune. Will protect from harm from others, inspires love and faithfulness and overall ensures a happy married life. It should be worn on 4th finger of right hand on Monday with silver. Weight should be 2, 4, 6, 9 grams. Being a cold stone it should be worn during bright nights.

3. *Coral:* Coral ensures material happiness, recovery from diseases indicated by Mars such as fever, cough, billious complaints, smallpox, chickenpox, headache, loss of vitality, piles, boils, measles, etc. In Hindi, the gem is called Moonga. It should be worn in silver or copper and be of 9, 11, 12 grams on Tuesday on 1st or 4th finger of right hand. It is a hot stone.

4. *Emerald:* Emerald or Panna is a hot gem. It increases intelligence and brain power, removes and cures fickle-mindedness, loss of memory, stammering, fear from souls and spirits, cools the harsh speech but reduces passions and sexual desires. Newly married couples should not use it as it impairs conjugal happiness due to reduction in sexual desires.

It is also useful for curing diarrhoea, dysentry, gastritic, peptic ulcer, asthma, insomnia, heart troubles, etc. It should be used in gold of 3, 5, 7 or 10 grams on 4th finger of right hand on Wednesday.

5. *Topaz:* Topaz or Pukhraj is a cold gem. It increases the power of penetrating vision, increases wealth, unlimited prosperity, life security, protects ones from poverty, removes adversity, misfortune and melancholy. Topaz cures diarrhoea, gastritis, ulcer, rheumatism, jaundice, insomnia, heart troubles, impotency, gout, arthritis, pain in knee joints, etc. Topaz should be worn in gold, on 1st finger of right hand on Thursday. The weight should be of 7 or 13 grams.

6. *Diamond:* Diamond or Hira is a hot gem. It creates goodness and removes evil and fearful thoughts in native. It improves financial conditions and blesses the native with comforts and peace of mind. Also cures diabetes, diseases of urine, of private parts, syphilis, skin and uterine diseases. It should be worn on 1st finger of right hand on Friday in gold or platinum. The weight should be 1/4 or 1/2 gram.

7. *Sapphire:* Sapphire or Neelam is a very cold gem. They are yellow or blue in colour. Removes evil effects of Saturn. It should be tested before use. It brings wealth, name and fame. Also gives good stamina, longevity and security in life. Can improve fertility in a barren woman. Best suited for joy, love and happiness. It cures fainting, fits, virility, mental disorder, deafness and baldness. It should be used on 2nd finger of right hand in gold or panch dhatu on Saturday and the weight is 5 or 7 grams.

8. *Hassonite:* Hassonite is the English name for Gomed which is cold in nature. It cures diseases caused by Rahu and Saturn. It also increases appetite, vitality, confers good health, wealth and happiness and all round prosperity. It should be used in silver on Saturday on 2nd finger of right hand. The weight should be 6, 11, 13 grams.

9. *Cat's Eye:* Cat's Eye or *Lahasanya* is too hot in nature. Useful for eradicating evil influences of Ketu and diseases caused by Mars. Prevents unexpected mishaps of life, cures mania, paralysis etc. Saves from accidents and secret enemies. For businessmen, it is a miraculous result-giver stone. Bestows wealth by secret means like horse racing, gambling, stock and share exchange market and speculations. It should be worn in gold on 2nd finger or 3rd finger of right hand on Thursday. The weight should be 3, 5 or 7 grams.

Colours

Colours are another way of propitiations and have remarkable effects. The author has analysed the effects of colours and put them in practice since years and have found remarkable effects. As an example let a Martian or Leo use constantly black colour or a Saturnian use constantly red colour, they will feel the evil effects.

There are seven main colours. Each colour has been assigned to each planet. These colours are Violet (Jupiter), Indigo (Saturn), Blue (Venus), Green (Moon), Yellow (Mercury), Orange (Sun) and Red (Mars). White is the mother of all colours and is assigned to Moon also.

Colour Therapy deals with use of colours. Colours have a great magnetic power on persons of all ages. Rainbow is nature's use of colours.

As every colour has modifying shades, one can undergo personality shades of changes within the same colour.

Vibratory Value of Colours

Now we shall explain the vibratory values of different colours. Each main colour has different shades known as mingled shades.

(A) 1. *Red:* Red is the colour of rashness, energy, of soldier, restlessness and revolution and anarchy. This colour has the greatest vibratory force and most powerful of all colours. Basically the persons are of materialistic mind.

People who like red colour are usually stout and strong with a robust outlook. It shows vitality and virility. Not headstrong but perfectly controllable. They are zealous, bold, determined, rash and have endurance. Courageous and sacrificing, passionate and optimistic, enthusiastic with high spirits. But such persons need guidance for their proper development in life. Red colour is a protector of ladies. Restows strong will power and courage. It is assigned to Mars. They should fast on Tuesday.

2. *Pink:* Persons liking pink colour are social, helpful to others, they have more love than admiration, are of mild nature without being jealous or malefic. They are sensitive, easily hurt, have depressions of short duration. Dark pink denotes that more depressive moods need to

be controlled. The lighter the shade of pink, the more loving, gentle and humane they are Bright pinks show buoyancy. Dull hues indicate glumness and gloominess.

3. *Crimson:* Such persons are optimistic, of high spirits, competitive nature, eager for success, ambitious and aggressiveness. In spite of the fact, that such persons have shortcomings, they have a bright future. Such persons are of affectionate nature and have capacity to sway opinions.

4. *Maroon:* Maroon colour has red vibrations. Such persons are of true fighting nature, strong, have purpose and restraint, can face many ups and downs of life with courage. They have a friendly nature, are affectionate and cooperative. The richer the maroon colour, the better and the vibratory influences. Too much of the brown shade makes one gloomy and selfish.

5. *Scarlet:* Such persons are of rash temperament, lack purpose and have restless moods, have a superficial nature, are selfish, volatile and vivacious.

6. *Brown:* Brown colour too has redness. Such persons are good followers and dependable. They know how to do and die without reasoning why. They do not enter into arguments, they either obey or rebel. Such persons should be handled reasonably and carefully with a sense of duty and discipline.

(B) 7. *Violet:* Violet colour is most soothing and harmonious for glory, grandeur, greatness and is effective for the nervous system. It promotes higher and nobler ideas. Such persons are fond of self-respect, can influence others, have literary, artistic or dramatic abilities, deep imagination and creative mind. They have profound longing for the mystical knowledge of nature. This colour helps in meditation and in increasing the power of concentration.

People liking violet colours are shy of any adverse remarks and fight for what they believe. They must end egotism, and vanity can prove to be the cause of their failure.

Voilet rays heal many diseases like neurotic, mental and nervous diseases, rheumatism, kidney troubles, etc. The colour is assigned to Jupiter.

8. *Lavender:* Lavender colour is a shade of violet colour. People with this vibration have a sweet nature. They are precise in their behaviour and demeanour, they have exact observance of forms. Such persons are disciplined and exacting in social dealings. To achieve their main object and goal, they ignore minor strifes; they are of affectionate nature.

(C) 9. *Indigo:* This ray is a mixture of more blue and less red. Such persons are more affectionate and less devoted. One becomes immune from fear and inhibition. Social help is their keynote. They are moody, calm and tranquil.

Mixture of other colours and tinges reduces the steadfast character of the blues. A strong tinge of grey creates uncertainty and even provides fears. A mixture of green with blue such as in some shades of turquoise indicates impetuousness. The colour is assigned to Saturn.

10. *Black:* Normally, the black colour in Astrology is assigned to Saturn. It is not a glum or gloomy colour. It is a symbol of formality and convention. It indicates dignity without false pride of dynamic action and profound thought. It is more genuine than showy, such persons are trustworthy, they are genuinely true but not showy. It exercises a great control on the subjects as well as on those who come into contact with it.

(D) 11. *Blue:* It is a cooling light, and has variable shades from lightest blue to darkest blue. It blends sensitivity with enthusiasm. Powerful for expressions. Such persons are generally lazy, fond of all comforts in life and sexy. The moods vary with changing shades. It rises to great heights of inspiration and descends to the bottoms of lowest perspiration.

Blue colour is for duty, devotion and dedication, such people make friends easily, they enjoy independence and self-sufficiency. It seeks higher things and deeper causes for life. It denotes dedication to nobler causes. This colour is assigned to Venus.

12. *Navy Blue:* It is strong dark colour. It shows trustworthiness and faithfulness, it also indicates tenacity of purpose. It denotes self-sufficiency with a spirit of give and take. Cooperativeness, strength and reliability are the keynotes of its character.

13. *Sky Blue:* It is a truly heavenly colour. Such people renunciate the world and dedicate their lives to humanity, they have unselfish motives dedicated to higher spiritual aspiration.

14. *Purple:* Purple is a royal blue colour. Such people command respect in higher society, have superior nature, prestige and power is their only aim in life. They hope to realise social importance.

(E) 15. *Yellow:* Yellow colour has been assigned to Mercury, the planet of intelligence. Such persons have robust character, are generous, intelligent, gentle and genius. One is of a scientific mind and has methods in all spheres and actions. The colour is of saints, mystics, artists and craftsmanship. Such persons are wise, creative and of inventive mind. Moody, optimistic and opportunist.

When yellow colour has a golden glow but a shade of dull paleness, intelligence is restrained by caution. One has many unpractical wishful thinkings.

· Dull yellow indicates selfishness and opportunism. Yellow-brown indicates moody mind and muddling; they achieve small things while hiding the big ones.

16. *Golden Glow:* It is an aura of deep inner understanding of life and the world. Such persons are highly intuitive and see things through and through. They see your character as in a mirror. They concentrate their energies on the lasting objects of the life.

(F) 17. *Green:* Green colour has been assigned to Moon. Such persons are even tempered and have a well balanced outlook, can mould themselves to circumstances and conditions. They are sentimental, sympathetic, fond of society and companion, over-zealous, take life too seriously. Such persons are slow in anger, and restrained by hesitation and thoughtfulness. They are firm and dogmatic, of strong will power, enthusiastic and optimistic. They should not be lazy and lethargic.

18. *Sea Green:* Sea green is darker than all green colours. It carries envy with strength. It is truly green-eyed. Towards yellow, green becomes a symbol of instability. Towards blue, it is an indication of excessive smartness.

19 *Olive Green:* Indicates dull and weak nature, finds excuses not to act. It has negative vibrations. It is evasive and impractical. Not a helpful colour for those who prefer it.

20. *Emerald Green:* It is a strong rich green colour. Its expression of aura is most volatile. One adapts oneself to most adverse

circumstances and character. One makes the best of the worst circumstances.

21. *Apple Green:* It is a colour of hopefulness and genuine expectations. It has optimistic vibrations. It indicates sympathy. Such persons are sentimental and warmly enthusiastic.

22. *White:* It is a mother colour and is assigned to Moon. It is a symbol of purity, such persons have a clear mind unmuddled by worldly affairs of greed and selfishness. The people who choose this colour in old age rather than in childhood or youth are false people who make a show of fastidiousness and physical cleanliness; they are critical of others who do not abide by social standards.

(G) 23. *Orange:* Orange colour is a dynamic derivative of red colour and has been assigned to Sun. It indicates high ambitions, people are proud, self contained, conceited and self-centred. They can influence others. They are high-minded and fully self-controlled. They are not obsessed with sexual affairs and are cool, if not cold and lack warmth in dealing with others. They have independent drive and are not dynamically social.

Such persons do meet with failures due to habits of if's and but's, they do not go out to their way to seek opportunity and popularity, overcome the opponents and oppositions of inventive skill and display sheer exuberance in their activities. They feel contended when they get what they want, act with self-confidence and courage. Their struggle in life is not restricted by laws of logic but rather with laws of love.

24. *Grey:* Grey colour indicates indecision and uncertainty, also false bravados but such people have self-confidence to face social challenges of prudery, they are firm in whatever they do and ignore public opinion. Grey with a silver tinge shows constancy and sincerity.

Colour Combinations

On the above basis, one can judge a fair measure of one's nature, his career and character from colour combination for which a person shows preference.

Colours for Signs

Each sign or Rasi is governed by its lord, otherwise known as a planet and accordingly each Rasi or sign has been allotted different colours.

In order to enjoy good luck, one should ascertain his Ascendant and use the colours as indicated in the following table.

Ascending Signs and colours

Ascending sign	Favourable colours	Colours to be avoided
1. Aries	Red, Copper, Yellow, Golden	Black
2. Taurus	Blue, Pink, Green and White	Red
3. Gemini	Green, Yellow, Purple, Blue, Pink	Red and Black
4. Cancer	Green, White, Cream, Red, Yellow	Blue
5. Leo	Orange, Red, Green	Black
6. Virgo	Green, White, Yellow and Emerald	Red, Blue and Black
7. Libra	Blue, Orange, White, Red	Green, Yellow
8. Scorpio	Yellow, Red, Cream, Orange	Blue, White and Green
9. Sagittarius	Violet, White, Cream., Orange, Light Blue and Emerald	Red, Pearl and Black
10. Capricorn	Indigo, White, Red, Blue, Black	Yellow, Cream
11. Aquarius	Indigo, Yellow, White, Cream	Orange, Blue, Green and Red
12. Pisces	Green, Violet, Red, Yellow, Rose Orange, Cream and White	Blue.

Colours and Birth Numbers

Select the colour for use as per your birth number for good luck. Use of colour should include dress, bedroom curtains, bedsheets, etc.

Birth No   Favourable colours

1. All shades of brown, light or dark and shades of yellow and gold colours.

2. All shades of green, darkest to lightest, also cream and white. Avoid red and black.

3. Use all shades of mauve, violet, pale or lilac shade of purple.

4. Use electric colours, namely blues, greys, electric blues and half shades. Avoid strong or positive colours of all kinds.

5. Light shades of all colours, especially light grey, white and glistening material. Never use dark colours.

6. All shades of blue, from light to dark navy but not electric blue. Also shades of rose or pink but not red, scarlet or crimson.

7. All shades of pale green, white, yellow and gold colours.

8. All shades of dark greys, dark blue, purple and black. Light and gaudy colours should be avoided.

9. All shades of red, rose, crimson, pink or red and purple. The darker or rich shades of these colours are best for them.

TANTRIK REMEDIES

Current definitions of Tantra as, "Sacred Writings of Hindus", "Scriptures of Sakta", "Collection of Magical Treatises" and the like, are either inaccurate and insufficient or by their generality useless. A type of such inaccurate statement characterised by the usual vagueness and indecision says that, "The Tantras are a latter development of the Puranic creed and written very much on the same lines as the Puranas."

But actually, the word Tantra has various meanings and amongst others Sastras generally, and therefore does not necessarily denote a religious scripture. The Sastra is stated to have been revealed by Lord Shiva as the specific scripture of the fourth or present kali age. This is the definition of Tantra according to the Sastras itself.

Lord Shiva, the Supreme, promulgates His teachings in the works known as Yamala, Damara. Siva Stutra and in the Tantras which exist in the form of dialogues between the Devotion and his Shakti, the Devi in her form as Parvati. According to Gayatri Tantra, the Deva Ganesa first preached the Tantra to Devayani on Mount Kailash, after he had himself received them from the mouth of Lord Shiva.

From the above discussions, one should understand that as per common belief Tantra is not a magic but a Sadhana and in this Sadhana the methods have been provided to ward off the worldly evils and troubles. A few such tested Mantras, Yantras, Tantras have been provided in detail in the author's books, *Practicals of Yantra* and *Practicals of Mantras and Tantras* Nefarious use of Tantric methods should always be discarded.

In Tantrik Sadhana, there are three ways to mitigate the evil effects:

1. Mantras-Prayer
2. Yantras
3. Tantras

We describe them briefly for the guidance of readers.

Mantras

"Prayer changeth the things" and Mantras are more superior than Yantras and Tantras. The persons who do not have wealth, education or wisdom but possess Mantra Sidhi are said to have everything. They can procure everything through Mantra. Through Mantras, you can control the calamities of life. It is the topmost sacred method. Each Mantra creates definite vibrations through its recitation method, belief and faith in the particular deity who is attracted towards Sadhaka. We provide only four Mantras. Consult the above books for more Mantras for various uses.

Use of Gayatri Mantra in Tantric: Gayatri Mantra has been held in the highest esteem in Hindu religion. This Mantra can be used in a Tantric way to solve one's problems, difficulties etc. by performing Havan or Homa of Gayatri Mantra with the following directions. The Mantra reads thus:

ॐ भूर्भुवः स्वः। तत्सवितुर् वरेण्यं भर्गो देवस्य
धीमहि धियो यो नः प्रचोदयात्॥

okbuwaha sanaha /Varenjnm/

"Om bhur bhawa savaha Tatsavetur Varaneum Bhargo Devesya. De Mahi Deyo yo na parchodyat".

In this Mantra after the words "Om Bhur bhawa savaha", the following words for the specific purposes shown against each should be added and then the whole Mantra recited. These specific words are called Samput. The Samput has a great value in Tantric and should be used carefully.

1. ॐ श्रीं ह्रीं श्रीं

This Samput is used for wealth and comforts. (Om Shreem Hreem-Shreem)

2. ॐ ऐं कलीं सौं:

This Samput is used for obtaining proficiency in words. (Om Aem Kaleem som).

3. ॐ श्रीं ह्रीं कलीं

One is blessed with progeny and

enjoys sexual bliss by use of this Samput. (Om Shreem Hreem Kaleem)

4. ॐ ऐं हीं कलीं   By the use of this Samput enemies are destroyed, troubles and worries vanish and the native is blessed with joy and happiness. (Om Aem Hreem Kaleem)

5. ॐ हीं   One recovers from illness through the use of this Samput. (Om Hreem)

6. ॐ औं हीं कलीं   One's hopes are fulfilled and the native is protected from evils (Om Oum Hreem Kaleem)

For Vashi Karan: In Pushy nakshatra, uproot the root of Punarnaka plant. Recite the Mantra 7 times and wear it on arm. All will be kind.

"ॐ नमो सर्वलोक वशेंकराय कुरु कुरु स्वाहा"

(Om Namo Sarvlok, vashi karaye, kuru kuru savaha).

For Wealth: This Mantra should be recited in a lonely place 21 thousand times. Homa must be performed with a mixture of sugar, rice and milk (kheer).

"ॐ ह्री कलीं श्रीं नमः"

(Om Hreem Kaleem Shreem Namaha)

To gain object: Om chimi chimi savaha

"ॐ चिमि चिमि स्वाहा"

Rise early in the morning; after ablutions purify the water for 7 times with the name of the person required to be put under your control. Drink this water. Repeat for 21 days, you will gain your object.

In Tantric Sadhana, Mantras are for *Shanti Karan,* viz. for cure of diseases, and warding off the malefic influence of planets. *Vashi karan* means to put under your control anybody. *Stambhan* is to stop a person from doing an evil and acting against you.

The fourth use is *Videshan* which causes differences between two persons or many. *Uchchattan* is known to distract the mind of a person from anything you wish. Sixth use of Mantra is *Maran* viz. these are death-inflicting Mantras by which you can kill anybody.

But nefarious use of Mantras is strictly prohibited.

Yantras

Technically speaking Yantra means an instrument, apparatus or talisman or a mystical diagram. Commonly it is mistaken as a magic which is a superstitious meaning of the term.

Yantra is not any magic but a path or technique through which you can attain your object and desires in the shortest way provided they are used as per instructions and directions. Yantra shakti is very wide, our Maha Rishis have practised and attained perfection in it. It is said that Devas reside in Yantras and without performing pooja of Yantra you cannot evoke the power of Yantra and get the desired results. Yantras include signs and writings coupled with Mantra pooja.

Yantras are used in many ways, viz. to wear on body, to keep at a place, or to do pooja of Yantras etc. They are prepared under definite guidelines on the proper day, time and place etc.

The most famous and effective Yantras as per our Sastras are:

1. Shri Yantra or Sri Chakra
2. Kali Yantra
3. Bagla mukhi Yantra
4. Mahamritanje Yantra
5. Tara Yantra
6. Shri Ganesh Yantra
7. Shri Bhairon Yantra
8. Shri Saraswati Yantra
9. Kuber Yantra
10. Sarvasidhi Yantra

Here we provide a few *Tested Yantras* from Hindu, Jain or Mulism cults for your information and use.

1. *For Love and Gain:* The Yantra must be written on Bhoj Patra or carved on stainless or copper plate. After pooja it should be kept on the body by the spiritualist. All persons will love you and no one will talk ill of you but instead will be helpful. It is a Mohammedan Yantra.

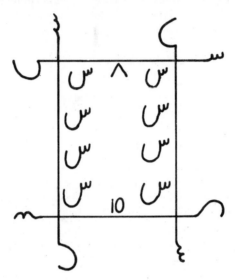

2. *To Control the Enemy:* This Yantra should be written on Bhoj patra. Sankhia and Hartal must be mixed and the Yantra should be

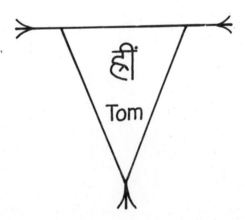

written with the wing of a crow. Write the name of the enemy in place of the word 'Tom'. Purify the Yantra through pooja. Take the bone of a man and put the yantra in the bone and bury it in the cremation ground. The enemy will come under control.

3. *Husband and Wife:* In case a husband is indifferent to his wife. The wife should tie this Yantra on her arm as well as on the arm of her husband or to his photo. Both will mutually agree.

٢٨٧

۴	٢	٢
١	٤	٩
٨	٣	٢

4. *To Remove the Influence of Evil Eye:* (i) When one is influenced by an evil eye, keep this Yantra on the body or around the neck, one will be cured.

مام ام ص ص د م م م مر د د ع ع

(ii) When a child does not read, hesitate to go to school use as above.

5. *For Barren Woman only:* This Yantra is quite useful for woman, who do not conceive. By the use of this Yantra, she will become pregnant. Write this Yantra on Bhoj Patra or Talpatra or on stainless plate with Ashat Gandh. Perform Pooja of Rudra or Rudra Kali and wear this Yantra on left arm, or waist or in neck. She will become pregnant.

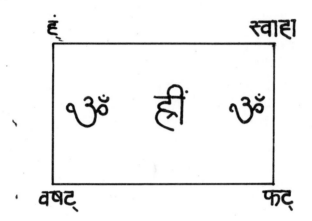

6. *Beesi Yantras:* Beesi Yantra is most famous and effective, provided it is prepared and pooja is performed according to rituals and with full faith. The Yantra is practised in all religions, Hindus, Buddhas, Parsis, Sikhs, Mohammedans etc. I have practised it extensively with good success.

There are various types of Yantras, written with Ashat Gandh on Bhoj Patra or carved on silver or stainless steel or copper plate and after pooja should be kept on body or worn around neck etc.

A few Yantras are shown. These Yantras are for wealth and happiness. Desires of sadhaka or user are fulfilled.

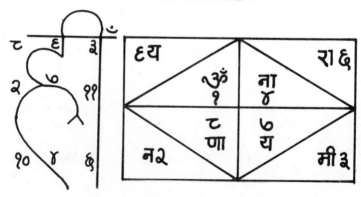

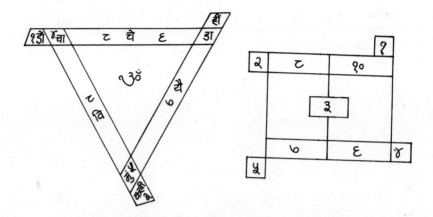

Mohammedan Beesi Yantras: These Yantras are written on Thursday with dhoop or looban while facing West and kept on the person. One will be blessed with health, wealth and happiness.

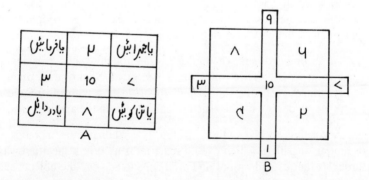

The Yantra marked A is found written on the Tomb of Mehmood Mian in Bhagdad Shariff whereas the Yantra marked B is written on Jama Masjid, Agra.

7. *To Create Quarrels*: Write this Yantra on Tuesday with the wing of an owl on an earthen piece obtained from the kiln of a pitcher maker. After that the Yantra must be thrown in the enemy's house. Quarrels will start in the house.

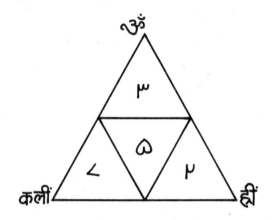

Note: About 550 effective Yantras have been provided in *Practicals of Yantras*

Tantra

Tantra word in Sastras means all that we know in detail about all Mantras and their use and how by its use we can protect people from fear etc. and do good service to them.

According to others, Tantra is a Sastra through which we deal with various aspects of life like pooja of Shiva Shakti and others, administrative methods, rules, methods of dealing with others and a Sastra which deals with the articles connected with the above points.

According to the author, Tantra is a sadhana or method or technique or path in which natural material is used in a specified way through Mantras under rules and directions to achieve the objects and desires. It does not touch your religion and faith, rather it strengthens it by way of pooja or prayer to your God and Deities.

The public at large understand Mantra, Yantra and Tantra as a magic or mysticism   [जादू-टोना]   and this misgiving in very deep-rooted in their minds. They feel that just as a magician performs miracles Tantra, Mantra and Yantras should also indicate like that, because in this material world everyone has many desires and is very egoistic in the fulfilment of his desires. But the people forget the law of nature which denotes that if you want to get anything, do struggle for that. People want shortcuts and that does not pay without spirituality. The path of spirituality is straight but you have to travel on it safely and methodically in a serious way.

Aagam is the word which Lord Shiva told Devi Parvati and which was accepted by Lord Vishnu. So the word originates from Lord Shiva which carries the sanctions of Lord Vishnu and which has further been carried to mankind through Devi Parvati, but the use of Tantra for nefarious purposes is prohibited.

Tantra, Yantra and Mantra are interconnected. Tantra cannot be successful without Mantra siddhi. Unless and otherwise both are not practised simultaneously, success cannot be achieved in Tantra.

So dear readers, understand this point precisely and understand Tantra as sadhana or practice and not as a magic. *Be careful and be warned.*

Tantra is being practised since ages by all religions and are called Jain Tantra, Buddha Tantra, Brahmin Tantra and Muslim Tantra.

We have only provided a few Tantras for the guidance and use of readers. For further detail read the author's book *Practicals of Mantras and Tantras*. Like Yantras, Tantra is used for various aspects of life.

1. *For Vashi Karan*: To enchant anybody, the following Tantra should be used. This is called Sarv Jan Vashi Karan. This also includes Mohan and Akarshan etc.

"ॐ नमो आदिपुरूषाय अमुकं आकर्षण कुरू कुरू स्वाहा।"

Mantra: "Om Namo Adipuruechaye *Amukam* Akarshan Kuru Kuru Savaha".

Recite this Mantra ten thousands times, you will have siddhi of Mantra. Purify articles for this purpose 108 times and use for the person by replacing the name in the Mantra with the word, *Amukam*. Its uses are with:

a. During Pushy nakshatra, make a powder of the root of Manjeeth. Put it on the head of anybody, who will be infatuated.

b. During Shukla Paksh on Sunday, take ashes from the cremation ground, mix your semen, ashes of burnt nails of your hand and feet. This powder must be preserved. As and when required, it should be given to any lady or man an eatable and they will come under your control.

c. The Meat of owl should be dried in shade. Anybody on whose head a pinch of it is thrown will be enchanted.

d. Mix ashes from the cremation ground with Braham Dandi. Throw this powder on anybody and they will be enchanted.

e. Procure the earth trodden on by a Brahmin, Cow, Ass and dog during Pushy nakshatra on Sunday. Mix them well. To infatuate anybody put a pinch of it on his/her head.

f. Cut the nails of hands and feet. Burn them and get the powder. Which must be purfied with the above Mantra. Mix it in any eatables and offer it to a lady/man who will be enchanted.

2. *Videshan*: Through Videshan Tantra, differences are created amongst friends, enemy, opponents, associations, etc.

These Tantras are used when a person creates troubles, obstacles, teases the other man and creates unhealthy atmosphere at home, and puts others to loss or inconvenience. In order to stop them from doing so, these Tantras are used to get relief. In self-defence you can use them.

"ॐ नमो नारायणाय अमुकामुकेन सह विद्वेषणं
कुरु कुरु स्वाहा।"

Mantra: "Om Namo Narayanay Amuk amukem Seh Videshan Kuru Kuru Svaha"

The Mantra must be recited for 21 days, one rosary daily. Change the word, *Amuk* with the name of the person. Then purify the articles with 108 Mantras and use them as directed hereunder:

a. The persons among whom you want to create differences. Fix the pointed wings of a sea bird on the doors of such persons after purifying them 108 times. There will be quarrels and separations between them.

b. Hair of a lady and clothes of a man must be burnt on Tuesday. The Ashes must be thrown on the heads of the couple, there will be quarrels between the two.

c. Hairs of a horse and a buffalo must be purified 108 times with the said Mantras. Wherever they are burnt, differences will be created.

d. Collect on Sunday the dust of the place where asses relax. Purify them, wherever this dust is thrown, Videshan will start at that place.

e. Early in the morning two flowers must be burnt in the fire for three days in the name of two persons, after purifying them. They will become enemies.

3. *Uchchatan*: Uchchatan Tantras are the methods through which the persons, animals, birds etc. are driven away from their places and professions. One is insulted and meets with failures, etc.

Actually these methods are used for enemies, maybe of country, or personal but mainly for self-protection which is allowed in our Sastras. Through these methods, the enemies are distracted in carrying out the actions which are against the interests of the Sadhaka.

Such purposes can be gained through Tantrik methods. No doubt the other person is troubled but one gains justice, so the methods must be applied for constructive ways only and only at the time of an emergency.

In Tantrik spirituality, this method dealing with ladies, men, enemies, friends and other people exists and should be used cautiously because it is very effective if performed with due rituals, faith and following full directions. *Uchchatan* means separation, extirpation, uprooting, dejection, sadness, indifference, bringing distraction in one's mind with the help of incarnations. On the basis of the above, following are a few Uchchatan Mantras and Tantras for use.

1. *Mantra:* "Om Shreem Shreem Shreem Svaha".

"ॐ श्रीं श्रीं श्रीं स्वाहा।"

Recite ten thousand times and purify articles 108 times with the Mantra.

a. Take a bone 12" long of a male and purify it with the above Mantra. Bury the bone in the house where Uchchatan is required.

b. Homa must be performed with the recitation of the name of the person considered for Uchchatan with the above Mantra, using the wings of a crow and owl. Ahuties in Homa must be 108 times on Tuesday or Saturday.

c. The ashes trodden by a she-ass must be purified with the above Mantra 21 times on Tuesday Noon. In any house, where thrown, it will be subjected to Uchchatan. Or the ashes trodden by the left foot of a man should be collected on Sunday.

d. Make powder of the head of an owl, purify with the above Mantra 21 times. Throw it on the head of an enemy. He will be afflicted by Uchchatan.

Other Uses

1. Half a shoe or the inside sole of the shoe of the enemy should be boiled in water on Sunday, Tuesday or Saturday, the enemy will become sick.

2. Ashes from the cremation ground must be brought on Monday or Tuesday and mixed with mustard. Homa must be performed with Aak wood 20 times with Mantra (Amukasya Han Han Svaha). Enemy will be troubled with serious illness.

" अमुकस्य हन हन स्वाहा"।

3. When the first tooth of a child breaks, it should be picked up before it falls on the ground. A lady who is not blessed with a

child must tie the tooth embedded in a copper or silver talisman on her left hand will be blessed with a child.

4. If the above talisman is tied around the waist of a woman, in a silver talisman, she will not conceive or abort.

5. When in extreme happiness, a man or woman weeps, then if these tears are sucked by anybody who is extremely worried the worries will vanish.

6. The umblical chord of a woman who has given birth to a male child first should be dried and preserved. Make a powder. If a childless woman takes it with any eatable, she will be blessed with a child.

7. The umblical chord of first male child should be dried and kept in a safe or purse. The man is blessed with wealth and is respected everywhere.

8. If a lady rubs the blood of her menses on her breasts, they will become hard.

9. If a person does not sleep during the night and if teeth of an ass are kept under the pillow, one will sleep comfortably.

10. The eye of an owl mixed with Kasturi, if put it on anybody will become your friend.

So with this, we request the readers to use the Astrology Mantra, Yantra and Tantra in all walks of life and allow the worries, evil effects of planets, etc. to be corrected through careful remedies for which they must consult the author or a competent astrologer.

OM TAT SAT

ASCENDANT TABLES

How to Use Lagna or Ascendant Tables

These lagna tables can be used to find a lagna on any date of any year for any time, day or night and for any place in India or Abroad without the help of any book.

The time indicated against each date and under each lagna denotes Beginning Time of the same lagna or Ending Time of preceding lagna. This is calculated according to the I.S.T. at 82 ∙°E.

The importance and correctness of lagna is known to every reader of Astrology. Lagna can be found at a glance for all purposes, like horoscopic prediction and Horary Astrology etc.

Method

1   In order to find a lagna or Ascendant for a place, first of all find the longitude of the place and note down whether it is East or West of 82 ∙°.

2. Find the difference between 82·°E and the longitude of the required place.

3. The difference may be multiplied by 4 minutes per degree.

4. This difference must be added to or subtracted from the time shown in the Table, if the place is West or East of 82·° respectively.

5. The time obtained thus is the time of Beginning of Lagna.

Example

Suppose we want to find a lagna at 9.30 p.m. at Chandigarh on 10th Mach, 1977.

Latitude of Chandigarh is 30·14° N and longitude is 76.53° E

Difference of longitude   = 82.30° minus 76·53°

= 5·37°

Difference of time   = (5·37°) 4mts/degree= 22.28° (West of 82·°)

Check the Table for the month of March. Against 10th March we find the time to be 20 hrs 33 mts. Adding 22 mts. 28 secs. we get 20 hrs. 55mts. 28secs. which is a beginning time of Tula or Libra lagna and the next time is 22 hrs 55 mts plus 22mts 28secs which is equal to 23 hrs 17mts 20 secs indicating ending time of Tula lagna.

In this way lagna can be found for any time, date and place.

BEGINNING OF LAGNAS I.S.T.

| | Posha | | | | JANUARY | | | | | Magha | | |
Date	Sagitt.	Capri.	Aquarius	Pisces	Aries	Taurus	Gemini	Cancer	Leo	Virgo	Libra	Scorpio
1	5-49	7-49	9-32	10-58	12-20	13-53	15-46	18-00	20-22	22-42	1-3	3-25
2	5-45	7-45	9-28	10-54	12-16	13-49	15-42	17-56	20-18	22-38	0-59	3-21
3	5-41	7-41	9-24	10-50	12-12	13-45	15-38	17-52	20-14	22-34	0-55	3-17
4	5-37	7-37	9-20	10-46	12-8	13-41	15-34	17-48	20-10	22-30	0-51	3-13
5	5-33	7-33	9-16	10-42	12-4	13-37	15-30	17-44	20-6	22-26	0-47	3-9
6	5-29	7-29	9-12	10-38	12-0	13-33	15-26	17-40	20-2	22-22	0-43	3-5
7	5-25	7-25	9-8	10-34	11-56	13-29	15-22	17-36	19-58	22-18	0-39	3-1
8	5-21	7-21	9-4	10-30	11-52	13-25	15-18	17-32	19-54	22-14	0-35	2-57
9	5-17	7-17	9-0	10-26	11-48	13-21	15-14	17-28	19-50	22-10	0-31	2-53
10	5-13	7-13	8-56	10-22	11-44	13-17	15-10	17-24	19-46	22-6	0-27	2-49
11	5-9	7-9	8-52	10-18	11-40	13-13	15-6	17-20	19-42	22-2	0-23	2-45
12	5-5	7-5	8-48	10-14	11-36	13-9	15-2	17-16	19-38	21-58	0-19	2-41
13	5-1	7-1	8-44	10-10	11-32	13-5	14-58	17-12	19-34	21-54	0-15	2-37
14	4-57	6-57	8-40	10-6	11-28	13-1	14-54	17-8	19-30	21-50	0-11	2-33
15	4-53	6-53	8-36	10-2	11-24	12-57	14-50	17-4	19-26	21-46	0-7	2-29
16	4-49	6-49	8-32	9-58	11-20	12-53	14-46	17-0	19-22	21-42	0-3	2-25
17	4-45	6-45	8-28	9-54	11-16	12-49	14-42	16-56	19-18	21-38	23-59	2-21
18	4-41	6-41	8-24	9-50	11-12	12-45	14-38	16-52	19-14	21-34	23-55	2-17
19	4-37	6-37	8-20	9-46	11-8	12-41	14-34	16-48	19-10	21-30	23-51	2-13
20	4-33	6-33	8-16	9-42	11-4	12-37	14-30	16-44	19-6	21-26	23-47	2-9
21	4-29	6-29	8-12	9-38	11-0	12-33	14-26	16-40	19-2	21-22	23-43	2-5
22	4-25	6-25	8-8	9-34	10-56	12-29	14-22	16-36	18-58	21-18	23-39	2-1
23	4-21	6-21	8-4	9-30	10-52	12-25	14-18	16-32	18-54	21-14	23-35	1-57
24	4-17	6-17	8-0	9-26	10-48	12-21	14-14	16-28	18-50	21-10	23-31	1-53
25	4-13	6-13	7-56	9-22	10-44	12-17	14-10	16-24	18-46	21-6	23-27	1-49
26	4-9	6-9	7-52	9-18	10-40	12-13	14-6	16-20	18-40	21-2	23-23	1-45
27	4-5	6-5	7-48	9-14	10-36	12-9	14-2	16-16	18-36	20-58	23-19	1-41
28	4-1	6-1	7-44	9-10	10-32	12-5	13-58	16-12	18-32	20-54	23-15	1-37
29	3-57	5-57	7-40	9-6	10-28	12-1	13-54	16-8	18-28	20-50	23-11	1-33
30	3-53	5-53	7-36	9-2	10-24	11-57	13-50	16-4	18-24	20-46	23-7	1-29

Date	Capri.	Aqua.	Pisces	Aries	Taurus	Gemini	Cancer	Leo	Virgo	Libra	Scorpio	Sagitt.
1	5-48	7-29	8-55	10-17	11-50	13-43	15-57	18-19	20-39	23-0	1-22	3-42
2	5-46	7-29	8-51	10-13	11-46	13-39	15-53	18-15	20-35	22-56	1-18	3-38
3	5-42	7-21	8-47	10-9	11-42	13-35	15-49	18-11	20-31	22-52	1-14	3-34
4	5-38	7-17	8-43	10-5	11-38	13-31	15-45	18-7	20-27	22-48	1-10	3-30
5	5-34	7-13	8-39	10-1	11-34	13-27	15-41	18-3	20-23	22-44	1-6	3-26
6	5-30	7-9	9-35	9-57	11-30	13-23	15-37	17-59	20-19	22-40	1-2	3-22
7	5-26	7-5	8-31	9-53	11-26	13-19	15-33	17-55	20-15	22-36	0-58	3-18
8	5-22	7-1	8-27	9-49	11-22	13-15	15-29	17-51	20-11	22-32	0-54	3-14
9	5-18	6-57	8-23	9-45	11-18	13-11	15-25	17-47	20-7	22-28	0-46	3-10
10	5-14	6-53	8-19	9-41	11-14	13-7	15-21	17-43	20-3	22-24	0-46	3-6
11	5-10	6-49	8-15	9-37	11-10	13-3	15-17	17-39	19-59	22-20	0-42	3-2
12	5-6	6-45	8-11	9-33	11-6	12-59	15-13	17-35	19-55	21-16	0-38	2-58
13	5-2	6-41	8-7	9-29	11-2	12-55	15-9	17-31	19-51	22-12	0-34	2-54
14	4-58	6-37	8-3	9-25	10-58	12-51	15-5	17-27	19-47	22-8	0-30	2-50
15	4-54	6-33	7-59	9-21	10-54	12-47	15-1	17-23	19-43	22-4	0-26	2-46
16	4-50	6-29	7-55	9-17	10-50	12-43	14-57	17-19	19-39	22-0	0-22	2-42
17	4-46	6-25	7-51	9-13	10-46	12-39	14-53	17-15	19-35	21-56	0-18	2-38
.18	4-42	6-21	7-47	9-9	10-42	12-35	14-49	17-11	19-31	21-52	0-14	2-34
19	4-38	6-17	7-43	9-5	10-38	12-31	14-45	17-7	19-27	21-48	0-10	2-30
20	4-34	6-13	7-39	9-1	10-34	12-27	14-41	17-3	19-23	21-44	0-6	2-26
21	4-30	6-9	7-35	8-57	10-30	12-23	14-37	16-59	19-19	21-40	0-2	2-22
22	4-26	6-5	7-31	8-53	10-26	12-19	14-33	16-55	19-15	21-36	23-58	2-18
23	4-22	6-1	7-27	8-49	10-22	12-15	14-29	16-51	19-11	21-32	23-54	2-14
24	4-18	5-57	7-23	8-45	10-18	12-11	14-25	16-47	19-7	21-28	23-50	2-10
25	4-14	5-53	7-19	8-41	10-14	12-7	14-21	16-43	19-3	21-24	23-46	2-6
26	4-10	5-49	7-15	8-37	10-10	12-3	14-17	16-39	18-59	21-20	23-42	2-2
27	4-6	5-45	7-11	8-33	10-6	11-59	14-13	16-35	18-55	21-16	23-38	1-58
28	4-2	5-41	7-7	8-29	10-2	11-55	14-9	16-31	18-51	21-12	23-34	1-54
29	3-58	5-37	7-3	8-25	9-58	11-51	14-5	16-27	18-47	21-8	23-30	1-50

| | Phagun | | | | | | MARCH | | | | Chaitra | |
Date	Aquarius	Pisces	Aries	Taurus	Gemini	Cancer	Leo	Virgo	Libra	Scorpio	Sagitt.	Capri.
1	5-42	7-4	8-26	8-59	11-52	14-6	16-28	18-48	21-9	32-31	1-51	3-55
2	5-38	7-0	8-22	9-55	11-48	14-2	16-24	18-44	21-5	23-27	1-47	3-51
3	5-34	6-56	8-18	9-51	11-44	13-58	16-20	18-40	21-1	23-23	1-43	3-47
4	5-30	6-52	8-14	9-47	11-40	13-54	16-16	18-36	20-57	23-19	1-39	3-43
5	5-26	6-48	8-10	9-43	11-36	13-50	16-12	18-32	20-53	23-15	1-35	3-39
6	5-22	6-44	8-6	9-39	11-32	13-46	16-8	18-28	20-49	23-11	1-31	3-35
7	5-18	6-40	8-2	9-35	11-28	13-42	16-4	18-24	20-45	23-7	1-27	3-31
8	5-14	6-36	7-58	9-31	11-24	13-38	16-0	18-20	20-41	23-3	1-23	3-27
9	5-10	6-32	7-54	9-27	11-20	13-34	15-56	18-16	20-37	22-59	1-19	3-23
10	5-6	6-28	7-50	9-23	11-16	13-30	15-52	18-12	20-33	22-55	1-15	3-19
11	5-2	6-24	7-46	9-19	11-12	13-26	15-48	18-8	20-29	22-51	1-11	3-15
12	4-58	6-20	7-42	9-15	11-8	13-22	15-44	18-4	20-25	22-47	1-7	3-11
13	4-54	6-16	7-38	9-11	11-4	13-18	15-40	18-0	20-21	22-43	1-3	3-7
14	4-50	6-12	7-34	9-7	11-0	13-14	15-36	17-56	20-17	22-39	12-59	3-3
15	4-46	6-8	7-30	9-3	10-56	13-10	15-32	17-52	20-13	22-35	12-55	2-59
16	4-42	6-4	7-26	8-59	10-52	13-6	15-28	17-48	20-9	22-31	12-51	2-55
17	4-38	6-0	7-22	8-55	10-48	13-2	15-24	17-44	20-5	22-27	12-47	2-51
18	4-34	5-56	7-18	8-51	10-44	12-58	15-20	17-40	20-1	22-23	12-43	2-47
19	4-30	5-52	7-14	8-47	10-40	12-54	15-17	17-36	19-57	22-19	12-39	2-43
20	4-26	5-48	7-10	8-43	10-36	12-50	15-12	17-32	19-53	22-15	12-35	2-39
21	4-22	5-44	7-6	8-39	10-32	12-46	15-8	17-28	19-49	22-11	12-31	
22	4-18	5-40	7-2	8-35	10-28	12-42	15-4	17-24	19-45	22-7	12-27	2-31
23	4-14	5-36	7-58	8-31	10-24	12-38	15-0	17-20	19-41	22-3	12-23	2-27
24	4-10	5-32	6-54	8-27	10-20	12-34	15-56	17-16	19-37	22-59	12-19	2-23
25	4-6	5-28	6-50	8-23	10-16	12-30	15-52	17-12	19-33	21-55	12-15	2-19
26	4-2	5-24	6-46	8-19	10-12	12-26	15-48	17-8	19-29	21-51	12-11	2-15
27	3-58	5-20	6-42	8-15	10-8	12-22	15-44	17-4	19-25	21-47	12-7	2-11
28	3-54	5-16	6-38	8-11	10-4	12-18	15-40	17-0	19-21	21-43	12-3	2-7
29	3-50	5-12	6-34	8-7	10-0	12-14	15-36	16-56	19-17	21-39	23-59	2-3
30	3-46	5-8	6-30	8-3	9-56	12-10	15-32	16-52	19-13	21-35	23-55	1-59
31	3-42											

Date	Pisces	Aries	Taurus	Gemini	Cancer	Leo	Virgo	Libra	Scorpio	Sagitt.	Capri.	Aquarius
1	5-1	6-23	7-56	9-49	12-3	14-25	16-45	19-6	21-28	23-48	1-52	3-35
2	4-57	6-19	7-52	9-45	11-59	14-21	16-41	19-2	21-24	23-44	1-48	3-31
3	4-53	6-15	7-48	9-41	11-54	14-17	16-37	18-58	21-20	23-40	1-44	3-27
4	4-49	6-11	7-44	9-37	11-51	14-13	16-33	18-54	21-16	23-36	1-40	3-23
5	4-45	6-7	7-40	9-33	11-47	14-9	16-29	18-50	21-12	23-32	1-36	3-19
6	4-41	6-3	7-36	9-29	11-43	14-5	16-25	18-46	21-8	23-28	1-32	3-15
7	4-37	5-59	7-32	9-25	11-39	14-1	16-21	18-42	21-4	23-24	1-28	3-11
8	4-33	5-55	7-28	9-21	11-35	13-57	16-17	18-38	21-0	23-20	1-24	3-7
9	4-29	5-51	7-24	9-17	11-31	13-53	16-13	18-34	20-56	23-16	1-20	3-3
10	4-25	5-47	7-20	9-13	11-27	13-49	16-9	18-30	20-52	23-12	1-16	2-59
11	4-21	5-43	7-16	9-9	11-23	13-45	16-5	18-26	20-48	23-8	1-12	2-55
12	4-17	5-39	7-12	9-5	11-19	13-41	16-1	18-22	20-44	23-4	1-8	2-51
13	4-13	5-35	7-8	9-1	11-15	13-37	15-57	18-18	20-40	23-0	1-4	2-47
14	4-9	5-31	7-4	8-57	11-11	13-33	15-53	18-14	20-36	22-56	1-0	2-43
15	4-5	5-27	7-0	8-53	11-7	13-29	15-49	18-10	20-32	22-52	0-57	2-39
16	4-1	5-23	6-56	8-49	11-3	13-25	15-45	18-6	20-28	22-48	0-53	2-35
17	3-57	5-19	6-52	8-45	10-59	13-21	15-41	18-2	20-24	22-44	0-49	2-31
18	3-53	5-15	6-48	8-41	10-55	13-17	15-37	17-58	20-20	22-40	0-45	2-27
19	3-49	5-11	6-44	8-37	10-51	13-13	15-33	17-54	20-16	22-36	0-41	2-23
20	3-45	5-5	6-40	8-33	10-47	13-9	15-29	17-50	20-12	22-32	0-37	2-19
21	3-41	5-3	6-36	8-29	10-43	13-5	15-25	17-46	20-8	22-28	0-33	2-15
22	3-37	4-59	6-32	8-25	10-39	13-1	15-21	17-42	20-4	22-24	0-29	2-11
23	3-33	4-55	6-28	8-21	10-35	12-57	15-17	17-38	20-0	22-20	0-25	2-7
24	3-27	4-51	6-24	8-17	10-31	12-53	15-13	17-34	19-56	22-16	0-21	2-3
25	3-25	4-47	6-20	8-13	10-27	12-49	15-9	17-30	19-52	22-12	0-17	1-59
26	3-21	4-43	6-16	8-9	10-23	12-45	15-5	17-26	19-48	22-8	0-13	1-55
27	3-17	4-39	6-12	8-5	10-19	12-41	15-1	17-22	19-44	22-4	0-9	1-51
28	3-13	4-35	6-8	8-1	10-15	12-37	14-57	17-18	19-40	22-0	0-5	1-47
29	3-9	4-31	6-4	8-57	10-11	12-33	14-53	17-14	19-36	21-56	0-1	1-43
30	3-6	1-20	6-1	7-54	10-8	12-30	14-50	17-11	19-33	21-53	23-57	1-40

Vaisakha   MAY   Jyeshta

Date	Aries	Tauris	Gemini	Cancer	Leo	Virgo	Libra	Scorpio	Sagitt.	Capri.	Aquari.	Pisces
1	4-24	5-57	7-50	10-4	12-26	14-46	17-7	19-29	21-49	23-53	1-36	3-2
2	4-20	5-52	7-46	10-0	12-22	14-42	17-3	19-25	21-45	23-49	1-32	2-58
3	4-16	5-49	7-42	9-56	12-18	14-38	16-59	19-21	21-41	23-45	1-28	2-54
4	4-12	5-45	7-38	9-52	12-14	14-34	16-55	19-17	21-37	23-41	1-24	2-50
5	4-8	5-41	7-34	9-48	12-10	14-30	16-51	19-13	21-33	23-37	1-20	2-46
6	4-4	5-37	7-30	9-44	12-6	14-26	16-47	19-9	21-29	23-33	1-16	2-42
7	4-0	5-33	7-26	9-40	12-2	14-22	16-43	19-5	21-25	23-29	1-12	2-38
8	3-56	5-29	7-22	9-36	11-58	14-18	16-39	19-1	21-21	23-25	1-8	2-34
9	3-52	5-25	7-18	9-32	11-54	14-14	16-35	18-57	21-17	23-21	1-4	2-30
10	3-48	5-21	7-14	9-28	11-50	14-10	16-31	18-53	21-13	23-17	1-0	2-26
11	3-44	5-17	7-10	9-24	11-46	14-6	16-27	18-49	21-9	23-13	0-56	2-22
12	3-40	5-13	7-6	9-20	11-42	14-2	16-23	18-45	21-5	23-9	0-52	2-18
13	3-36	5-9	7-2	9-16	11-38	13-58	16-19	18-41	21-1	23-5	0-48	2-14
14	3-32	5-5	6-58	9-12	11-34	13-54	16-15	18-37	20-57	23-1	0-44	2-10
15	3-28	5-1	6-54	9-8	11-30	13-50	16-11	18-33	20-53	22-57	0-40	2-6
16	3-24	4-57	6-50	9-4	11-26	13-46	16-7	18-29	20-49	22-53	0-36	2-2
17	3-20	4-53	6-46	9-0	11-22	13-42	16-3	18-25	20-45	22-49	0-32	1-58
18	3-16	4-49	6-42	8-56	11-18	13-38	15-59	18-21	20-41	22-45	0-28	1-54
19	3-12	4-45	6-38	8-52	11-14	13-34	15-55	18-17	20-37	22-41	0-24	1-50
20	3-8	4-41	6-34	8-48	11-10	13-30	15-51	18-13	20-33	22-37	0-20	1-46
21	3-4	4-37	6-30	8-44	11-6	13-26	15-47	18-9	20-29	22-33	0-16	1-42
22	3-0	4-33	6-26	8-40	11-2	13-22	15-43	18-5	20-25	22-29	0-12	1-38
23	2-56	4-29	6-22	8-36	10-58	13-18	15-39	18-1	20-21	22-25	0-8	1-34
24	2-52	4-25	6-18	8-32	10-54	13-14	15-35	17-57	20-17	22-21	0-4	1-30
25	2-48	4-21	6-14	8-28	10-50	13-10	15-31	17-53	20-13	22-17	0-0	1-26
26	2-44	4-17	6-10	8-24	10-46	13-6	15-27	17-49	20-9	22-13	23-56	1-22
27	2-40	4-13	6-6	8-20	10-42	13-2	15-23	17-45	20-5	22-9	23-52	1-18
28	2-36	4-9	6-2	8-16	10-38	12-58	15-19	17-41	20-1	22-5	23-48	1-14
29	2-32	4-5	5-58	8-12	10-34	12-54	15-15	17-37	19-57	22-1	23-44	1-10
30	2-28	4-1	5-54	8-8	10-30	12-50	15-11	17-33	19-53	21-57	23-40	1-6
31	2-24	3-57	5-50	8-4	10-26	12-46	15-7	17-29	19-49	21-53	23-36	1-2

Date	Taurus	Gemini	Cancer	Leo	Virgo	Libra	Scorpio	Sagitt.	Capri.	Aqua.	Pisces	Aries
1	3-54	5-47	8-1	10-23	12-43	15-4	17-26	19-46	21-50	23-33	0-59	2-21
2	3-50	5-43	7-57	10-19	12-39	15-0	17-22	19-42	21-46	23-29	0-55	2-17
3	3-46	5-39	7-53	10-15	12-35	14-56	17-18	19-38	21-42	23-25	0-51	2-13
4	3-42	5-35	7-49	10-11	12-31	14-52	17-14	19-34	21-38	23-21	0-47	2-9
5	3-38	5-31	7-45	10-7	12-27	14-48	17-10	19-30	21-34	23-17	0-43	2-5
6	3-34	5-27	7-41	10-3	12-23	14-44	17-6	19-26	21-30	23-13	0-39	2-1
7	3-30	5-23	7-37	9-59	12-19	14-40	17-2	19-22	21-26	23-9	0-35	1-57
8	3-26	5-19	7-33	9-55	12-15	14-36	16-58	19-18	21-22	23-5	0-31	1-53
9	3-22	5-15	7-29	9-51	12-11	14-32	16-54	19-14	21-18	23-1	0-27	1-49
10	3-18	5-11	7-25	9-47	12-7	14-28	16-50	19-10	21-14	22-57	0-23	1-45
11	3-14	5-7	7-21	9-43	12-3	14-24	16-46	19-6	21-10	22-53	0-19	1-41
12	3-10	5-3	7-17	9-39	11-59	14-20	16-42	19-2	21-6	22-49	0-15	1-37
13	3-6	4-59	7-13	9-35	11-55	14-16	16-38	18-58	21-2	22-45	0-11	1-33
14	3-2	4-55	7-9	9-31	11-51	14-12	16-34	18-54	20-58	22-41	0-7	1-29
15	2-59	4-51	7-5	9-27	11-47	14-8	16-30	18-51	20-55	22-38	0-4	1-25
16	2-55	4-47	7-1	9-23	11-43	14-4	16-27	18-47	20-5	23-34	0-0	1-22
17	2-51	4-43	6-58	9-19	11-39	14-0	16-23	18-43	20-47	22-30	23-36	1-18
18	2-47	4-39	6-54	9-15	11-35	13-37	16-19	18-39	20-43	22-26	23-52	1-14
19	2-43	4-35	6-50	9-11	11-31	13-33	16-15	18-35	20-39	22-22	23-48	1-10
20	2-39	4-31	6-46	9-7	11-27	13-49	16-11	18-31	20-35	22-18	23-44	1-6
21	2-35	4-27	6-42	9-3	11-23	13-45	16-7	11-27	20-31	22-14	23-40	1-2
22	2-31	4-23	6-38	9-0	11-19	13-41	16-3	18-23	20-27	22-10	23-36	0-58
23	2-27	4-19	6-34	8-56	11-15	13-37	15-59	18-19	20-23	22-6	23-32	0-54
24	2-23	4-15	6-30	8-52	11-11	13-33	15-55	18-15	20-19	22-2	23-28	0-51
25	2-19	4-11	6-26	8-48	11-7	13-30	15-52	18-12	20-15	21-59	23-25	0-47
26	2-15	4-7	6-22	8-44	11-3	13-26	15-48	18-8	20-12	21-55	23-21	0-43
27	2-12	4-3	6-18	8-40	11-1	13-22	15-44	18-4	20-8	21-51	23-17	0-39
28	2-8	3-59	6-14	8-36	10-57	13-18	15-40	18-0	20-8	21-47	23-13	0-35
29	2-4	3-55	6-10	8-32	10-53	13-14	15-36	17-56	20-00	21-43	23-9	0-31
30	2-0	3-52	6-6	8-28	10-49	13-10	15-33	17-53	19-56	21-39	23-5	0-27

Asarh JULY Sarvana

Date	Gemini	Cancer	Leo	Virgo	Libra	Scorpio	Sagitt.	Capri.	Aquari.	Pisces	Aries	Taurus
1	3-50	6-4	8-26	10-46	13-7	15-29	17-49	19-53	21-36	23-02	0-24	1-57
2	3-46	6-0	8-22	10-42	13-3	15-25	17-45	19-49	21-32	22-58	0-20	1-53
3	3-42	5-56	8-18	10-38	12-59	15-21	17-41	19-45	21-28	22-54	0-16	1-49
4	3-38	5-52	8-14	10-34	12-55	15-17	17-37	19-41	21-24	22-50	0-12	1-45
5	3-34	5-48	8-10	10-30	12-51	15-13	17-33	19-37	21-20	22-46	0-8	1-41
6	3-30	5-44	8-6	10-26	12-49	15-9	17-29	19-33	21-18	22-42	0-4	1-37
7	3-26	5-40	8-2	10-22	12-45	15-5	17-25	19-29	21-14	22-38	0-0	1-33
8	3-22	5-36	7-58	10-18	12-41	15-1	17-21	19-25	21-10	22-34	23-56	1-29
9	3-18	5-32	7-54	10-14	12-37	14-57	17-17	19-21	21-6	22-30	23-52	1-25
10	3-14	5-28	7-50	10-10	12-33	14-53	17-13	19-17	21-2	22-26	23-48	1-21
11	3-10	5-24	7-46	10-6	12-29	14-49	17-9	19-13	20-56	22-22	23-44	1-17
12	3-6	5-20	7-42	10-2	12-25	14-45	17-5	19-9	20-52	22-18	23-40	1-13
13	3-2	5-16	7-38	9-58	12-21	14-41	17-1	19-5	20-48	22-14	23-36	1-9
14	2-58	5-12	7-34	9-54	12-17	14-37	16-57	19-1	20-44	22-10	23-32	1-5
15	2-54	5-8	7-30	9-50	12-13	14-33	16-53	18-57	20-40	22-6	23-28	1-1
16	2-50	5-4	7-26	9-46	12-9	14-29	16-49	18-54	20-36	22-2	23-24	0-58
17	2-46	5-1	7-22	9-42	12-5	14-25	16-45	18-50	20-32	21-59	23-20	0-54
18	2-42	4-57	7-18	9-38	12-1	14-21	16-41	18-46	20-28	21-55	23-16	0-50
19	2-38	4-53	7-14	9-34	11-56	14-17	16-37	18-42	20-24	21-51	23-12	0-46
20	2-34	4-49	7-10	9-30	11-52	14-13	16-33	18-38	20-20	21-47	23-8	0-42
21	2-30	4-45	7-6	9-26	11-48	14-9	16-29	18-34	20-16	21-43	23-4	0-38
22	2-26	4-41	7-2	9-22	11-44	14-5	16-25	18-30	20-12	21-39	23-0	0-34
23	2-22	4-37	6-59	9-18	11-40	14-1	16-21	18-26	20-8	21-35	22-57	0-30
24	2-18	4-33	6-55	9-14	11-36	13-58	16-17	18-22	20-4	21-31	22-53	0-26
25	2-14	4-29	6-51	9-10	11-32	13-54	16-13	18-18	20-0	21-27	22-49	0-22
26	2-10	4-25	6-47	9-6	1-1-28	13-50	16-9	18-14	19-57	21-23	22-45	0-18
27	2-6	4-21	6-43	9-3	11-24	13-46	16-5	18-10	19-53	21-19	22-41	0-14
28	2-2	4-17	6-39	8-59	11-20	13-42	16-1	18-6	19-49	21-15	22-37	0-10
29	1-59	4-13	6-35	8-55	11-16	13-38	15-58	18-2	19-49	21-11	22-33	0-6
30	1-55	4-9	6-31	8-51	11-12	13-34	15-54	17-58	19-41	21-7	22-29	0-2
31	1-51	4-5	6-27	8-47	11-8	13-30	15-50	17-54	19-37	21-3	22-25	23-58

Date	Cancer	Leo	Virgo	Libra	Scorpio	Sagitt.	Caparic.	Aquarius	Pisces	Aries	Taurus	Gemini
1	4-2	6-24	8-44	11-5	13-27	15-47	17-51	19-34	21-00	22-55	23-55	1-48
2	3-58	6-20	8-40	11-1	13-23	15-43	17-47	19-30	20-56	22-51	23-51	1-44
3	3-54	6-16	8-36	10-57	13-19	15-39	17-43	19-26	20-52	22-47	23-47	1-40
4	3-50	6-12	8-32	10-53	13-15	15-35	17-39	19-22	20-48	22-43	23-43	1-36
5	3-46	6-8	8-28	10-49	13-11	15-31	17-35	19-18	20-44	22-39	23-39	1-32
6	3-42	6-4	8-24	10-45	13-7	15-27	17-31	19-14	20-40	22-35	23-35	1-28
7	3-38	6-0	8-20	10-41	13-3	15-23	17-27	19-10	20-36	22-31	23-31	1-24
8	3-34	5-56	8-16	10-37	12-59	15-19	17-23	19-6	20-32	22-27	23-27	1-20
9	3-30	5-52	8-12	10-33	12-55	15-15	17-19	19-2	20-28	22-23	23-23	1-16
10	3-26	5-48	8-8	10-29	12-51	15-11	17-15	18-58	20-24	22-19	23-19	1-12
11	3-22	5-44	8-4	10-25	12-47	15-7	17-11	18-54	20-20	22-15	23-15	1-8
12	3-18	5-40	8-0	10-21	12-43	15-3	17-7	18-50	20-16	22-11	23-11	1-4
13	3-14	5-36	7-56	10-17	12-39	14-59	17-3	18-46	20-12	22-7	23-7	1-0
14	3-10	5-32	7-52	10-13	12-35	14-55	16-59	18-42	20-8	22-3	23-3	0-56
15	3-6	5-28	7-48	10-9	12-31	14-51	16-55	18-38	20-4	22-59	22-59	0-52
16	3-2	5-24	7-44	10-5	12-28	14-48	16-51	18-34	20-0	22-56	22-56	0-48
17	2-59	5-20	7-40	10-1	12-24	14-44	16-48	18-30	19-57	22-52	22-52	0-44
18	2-55	5-16	7-36	9-58	12-20	14-40	16-44	18-26	19-53	22-48	22-48	0-41
19	2-51	5-12	7-32	9-54	12-16	14-36	16-40	18-22	19-49	22-44	22-44	0-37
20	2-47	5-8	7-28	9-50	12-12	14-32	16-36	18-18	19-45	22-40	22-40	0-33
21	2-43	5-4	7-24	9-46	12-8	14-28	16-32	18-14	19-41	22-36	22-36	0-29
22	2-39	5-0	7-20	9-42	12-4	14-24	16-28	18-10	19-37	22-32	22-32	0-25
23	2-35	4-57	7-16	9-38	12-0	14-20	16-24	18-6	19-33	22-28	22-28	0-21
24	2-31	4-53	7-12	9-34	11-56	14-16	16-20	18-2	19-29	22-24	22-24	0-17
25	2-27	4-49	7-8	9-30	11-52	14-12	16-16	17-59	19-25	22-20	22-20	0-13
26	2-23	4-45	7-4	9-26	11-48	14-8	16-12	17-55	19-21	22-16	22-16	0-9
27	2-19	4-41	7-1	9-22	11-44	14-4	16-8	17-51	19-17	22-12	22-12	0-5
28	2-15	4-37	6-57	9-18	11-40	14-0	16-4	17-47	19-13	22-8	22-8	0-1
29	2-11	4-33	6-53	9-14	11-36	13-57	16-0	17-44	19-9	22-4	22-4	23-57
30	2-7	4-30	6-49	9-10	11-32	13-53	15-57	17-40	19-5	22-1	22-1	23-54
31	2-3	4-26	6-45	9-6	11-28	13-49	15-53	17-36	19-1	21-57	21-57	23-50

Date	Leo	Virgo	Libra	Scorpio	Sagitt.	Capri.	Aquar.	Pisces	Aries	Taurus	Gemini	Cancer
1	4-23	6-43	9-4	11-26	13-46	15-50	17-33	18-59	20-21	21-54	23-47	2-1
2	4-19	6-39	9-0	11-22	13-42	15-46	17-29	18-55	20-17	21-50	23-43	1-51
3	4-15	6-35	8-56	11-18	13-38	15-42	17-25	18-51	20-13	21-46	23-39	1-53
4	4-11	6-31	8-52	11-14	13-34	15-38	17-21	18-47	20-9	21-42	23-35	1-49
5	4-7	6-27	8-48	11-10	13-30	15-34	17-17	18-43	20-5	21-38	23-31	1-45
6	4-3	6-23	8-44	11-6	13-26	15-30	17-13	18-39	20-1	21-34	23-27	1-41
7	3-59	6-19	8-40	11-2	13-22	15-26	17-9	18-35	19-57	21-30	23-23	1-37
8	3-55	6-15	8-36	11-2	13-18	15-22	17-5	18-31	19-53	21-26	23-19	1-33
9	3-51	6-11	8-32	10-54	13-14	15-18	17-1	18-27	19-49	21-22	23-15	1-29
10	3-47	6-7	8-28	10-50	13-10	15-14	16-57	18-23	19-45	21-18	23-1	1-25
11	3-43	6-3	8-24	10-46	13-6	15-10	16-53	18-19	19-41	21-14	23-7	1-21
12	3-39	5-59	8-20	10-42	13-2	15-6	16-49	18-15	19-37	21-10	23-3	1-17
13	3-35	5-55	8-16	10-38	12-58	15-4	16-45	18-11	19-33	21-6	22-59	1-5
14	3-31	5-51	8-12	10-34	12-54	15-2	16-41	18-7	19-28	21-2	22-55	1-2
15	3-27	5-47	8-8	10-30	12-50	14-58	16-37	18-3	19-25	20-58	22-51	0-58
16	3-23	5-43	8-4	10-26	12-46	14-54	16-37	18-00	19-21	20-54	22-47	0-54
17	3-20	5-39	8-0	10-22	12-42	14-50	16-29	17-56	19-17	20-50	22-43	0-51
18	3-16	5-35	7-57	10-18	12-38	14-46	16-25	17-52	19-13	20-46	22-39	0-46
19	3-12	5-31	7-53	10-14	12-34	14-42	16-21	17-48	19-9	20-42	22-35	0-42
20	3-8	5-27	7-49	10-10	12-30	14-38	16-17	17-44	19-5	20-38	22-31	0-38
21	3-4	5-23	7-45	10-6	12-26	14-34	16-13	17-40	19-1	20-34	22-27	0-34
22	3-0	5-19	7-41	10-2	12-22	14-30	16-9	17-36	18-58	20-30	22-23	0-30
23	2-56	5-15	7-37	9-59	12-18	14-26	16-5	17-32	18-54	20-26	22-19	0-26
24	2-52	5-11	7-33	9-55	12-14	14-22	16-1	17-28	18-50	20-22	22-15	0-22
25	2-48	5-7	7-29	9-51	12-10	14-18	15-58	17-24	18-46	20-18	22-11	0-18
26	2-44	5-3	7-25	9-47	12-6	14-14	15-54	17-20	18-42	20-14	22-8	0-14
27	2-40	5-0	7-21	9-43	12-2	14-10	15-50	17-16	18-36	20-10	22-4	0-10
28	2-36	4-56	7-17	9-39	11-59	14-6	15-46	17-12	18-31	20-6	22-0	0-6
29	2-32	4-52	7-13	9-35	11-55	14-2	15-42	17-8	18-30	20-2	-21-56	0-2
30	2-28	4-48	7-9	9-31	11-51	13-55	15-38	17-4	18-26	19-59	21-52	23-58

Date	Virgo	Libra	Scorpio	Sagitt.	Capri.	Aquarius	Pisces	Aries	Taurus	Gemini	Cancer	Leo
1	4-45	7-6	9-28	11-48	13-52	15-35	17-1	18-28	19-56	21-49	0-3	2-25
2	4-41	7-2	9-24	11-44	13-48	15-31	16-57	18-19	19-52	21-45	23-59	2-21
3	4-37	6-58	9-20	11-40	13-44	15-27	16-53	18-15	19-48	21-41	23-55	2-17
4	4-33	6-54	9-16	11-36	13-40	15-23	16-49	18-11	19-44	21-37	23-51	2-13
5	4-29	6-50	9-12	11-32	13-36	15-19	16-45	18-7	19-40	21-33	23-47	2-9
6	4-25	6-46	9-8	11-28	13-32	15-15	16-41	18-3	19-36	21-29	23-43	2-5
7	4-21	6-42	9-4	11-24	13-28	15-11	16-37	17-59	19-32	21-25	23-39	2-1
8	4-17	6-38	9-0	11-20	13-24	15-11	16-33	17-55	19-28	21-21	23-35	1-57
9	4-13	6-34	8-56	11-16	13-20	15-3	16-29	17-51	19-24	21-17	23-31	1-53
10	4-9	6-30	8-52	11-12	13-16	14-59	16-25	17-47	19-20	21-13	23-27	1-49
11	4-5	6-26	8-48	11-8	13-12	14-55	16-21	17-43	19-16	21-9	23-23	1-45
12	4-1	6-22	8-44	11-4	13-8	14-51	16-17	17-39	19-12	21-5	23-19	1-41
13	3-57	6-18	8-40	11-0	13-4	14-47	16-13	17-35	19-8	21-1	23-15	1-37
14	3-53	6-14	8-36	10-56	13-0	14-43	16-9	17-31	19-4	20-57	23-11	1-33
15	3-49	6-10	8-32	10-52	12-56	14-39	16-5	17-27	19-0	20-53	23-7	1-29
16	3-45	6-6	8-28	10-48	12-52	14-35	16-1	17-23	18-56	20-49	23-3	1-25
17	3-42	6-3	8-24	10-44	12-49	14-32	15-58	17-20	18-53	20-45	23-0	1-22
18	3-38	5-59	8-21	10-41	12-45	14-28	15-54	17-16	18-49	20-41	22-56	1-18
19	3-34	5-55	8-17	10-37	12-41	14-24	15-50	17-12	18-45	20-38	22-52	1-14
20	3-30	5-51	8-13	10-33	12-37	14-20	15-46	17-8	18-41	20-34	22-48	1-10
21	3-26	5-47	8-9	10-29	12-33	14-16	15-42	17-4	18-37	20-30	22-44	1-6
22	3-22	5-43	8-5	10-25	12-29	14-12	15-38	17-00	18-33	20-26	22-40	1-2
23	3-18	5-39	8-1	10-21	12-25	14-8	15-34	16-56	18-29	20-22	22-36	0-58
24	3-14	5-35	7-57	10-17	12-21	14-4	15-30	16-52	18-25	20-18	22-32	0-54
25	3-10	5-31	7-53	10-13	12-17	14-00	15-26	16-48	18-21	20-14	22-28	0-50
26	3-6	5-27	7-49	10-9	12-13-	13-56	15-22	16-44	18-17	20-10	22-24	0-46
27	3-2	5-23	7-45	10-9	12-9	13-52	15-18	16-40	18-13	20-6	22-20	0-42
28	2-58	5-19	7-41	10-5	12-5	13-48	15-14	16-36	18-9	20-2	22-16	0-38
29	2-54	5-15	7-37	9-57	12-1	13-44	15-10	16-32	18-5	19-58	22-12	0-34
30	2-50	5-11	7-33	9-53	11-57	13-40	15-6	16-28	18-1	19-54	22-8	0-30
31	2-46	5-7	7-29	9-49	11-53	13-36	15-02	16-24	17-57	19-50	22-4	0-26

Kartika   NOVEMBER   Maghsar

Date	Libra	Scorpio	Sagitt.	Capri.	Aquari.	Pisces	Aries	Taurus	Gemini	Cancer	Leo	Virgo
1	5-4	7-26	9-46	11-50	13-33	14-59	16-21	17-54	19-4	22-1	0-23	2-43
2	5-00	7-22	9-42	11-46	13-29	14-55	16-17	17-50	19-43	21-57	0-19	2-39
3	4-56	7-18	9-38	11-42	13-25	14-51	16-13	17-46	19-39	21-53	0-15	2-35
4	4-52	7-14	9-33	11-38	13-21	14-47	16-9	17-42	19-35	21-49	0-11	2-31
5	4-48	7-10	9-30	11-34	13-17	14-43	16-5	17-38	19-31	21-45	0-7	2-27
6	4-44	7-6	9-26	11-30	13-13	14-39	16-1	17-34	19-27	21-41	0-3	2-23
7	4-36	7-8	9-22	11-26	13-9	14-35	15-57	17-30	19-23	21-37	23-59	2-19
8	4-36	7-58	9-18	11-22	13-5	14-31	15-53	17-26	19-19	21-33	23-55	2-15
9	4-32	7-54	9-14	11-18	13-1	14-27	15-49	17-22	19-15	21-29	23-51	2-11
10	4-28	6-50	9-10	11-14	12-57	14-23	15-45	17-18	19-11	21-25	23-47	2-7
11	4-24	6-46	9-6	11-10	12-53	14-19	15-41	17-14	19-7	21-21	23-43	2-3
12	4-20	6-42	9-2	11-6	12-49	14-15	15-37	17-10	19-3	21-17	23-39	1-59
13	4-16	6-38	8-58	11-2	12-45	14-11	15-33	17-6	18-59	21-13	23-35	1-55
14	4-12	6-34	8-54	10-58	12-41	14-7	15-29	17-2	18-55	21-9	23-31	1-51
15	4-8	6-30	8-50	10-54	12-37	14-3	15-25	16-58	18-51	21-5	23-27	1-47
16	4-5	6-27	8-47	10-51	12-34	14-0	15-22	16-55	18-48	21-2	23-23	1-44
17	4-1	6-23	8-43	10-47	12-30	13-56	15-18	16-51	18-44	20-58	23-19	1-40
18	3-57	6-19	8-39	10-41	12-26	13-52	15-13	16-47	18-40	20-54	23-15	1-36
19	3-53	6-15	8-35	10-39	12-22	13-48	15-10	16-43	18-36	20-50	23-11	1-32
20	3-49	6-11	8-31	10-35	12-18	13-44	15-6	16-39	18-32	20-46	23-7	1-28
21	3-45	6 7	8-27	10-31	12-14	13-40	15-2	16-35	18-28	20-42	23-3	1-24
22	3-41	6-3	8-23	10-27	12-10	13-36	14-58	16-31	18-24	20-38	23-0	1-20
23	3-37	5-59	8-19	10-23	12-6	13-32	14-54	16-27	18-20	20-34	22-56	1-16
24	3-33	5-55	8-15	10-19	12-2	13-28	14-50	16-23	18-16	20-30	22-52	1-12
25	3-29	5-51	8-11	10-15	11-58	13-24	14-46	16-19	18-12	20-26	22-52	1-8
26	3-25	5-47	8-7	10-11	11-54	13-20	14-42	16-15	18-8	20-22	22-48	1-4
27	3-21	5-43	8-3	10-7	11-50	13-16	14-38	16-11	18-4	20-18	22-44	1-0
28	3-17	5-39	7-59	10-3	11-46	13-12	14-34	16-7	18-0	20-14	22-40	1-56
29	3-18	5-35	7-55	9-59	11-42	13-8	14-30	16-3	17-56	20-10	22-36	1-52
30	3-9	5-31	7-51	9-55	11-38	13-4	14-26	15-59	17-52	20-6	22-32	1-48

Date	Scorpio	Sagitt.	Capri.	Aquarius	Pisces	Aries	Taurus ·	Gemini	Cancer	Leo	Virgo	Libra
1	5-28	7-48	9-52	11-35	13-1	14-23	15-56	17-49	20-3	22-25	0-45	3-6
2	5-24	7-44	9-48	11-31	12-57	14-19	15-52	17-45	19-59	22-21	0-41	3-2
3	5-20	7-40	9-44	11-27	12-53	14-15	15-48	17-41	19-55	22-17	0-37	2-58
4	5-16	7-36	9-40	11-23	12-49	14-11	15-44	17-37	19-51	22-13	0-33	2-54
5	5-12	7-32	9-36	11-19	12-45	14-7	15-40	17-33	19-47	22-9	0-29	2-50
6	5-8	7-28	9-32	11-15	12-41	14-3	15-36	17-29	19-43	22-5	0-25	2-46
7	5-4	7-24	9-28	11-11	12-37	13-59	15-32	17-25	19-39	22-1	0-21	2-42
8	5-0	7-20	9-24	11-7	12-33	13-55	15-28	17-21	19-45	21-57	0-17	2-38
9	4-56	7-16	9-20	11-3	12-29	13-51	15-24	17-17	19-31	21-53	0-13	2-34
10	4-52	7-12	9-16	10-59	12-25-	13-47	15-20	17-13	19-27	21-49	0-9	2-30
11	4-48	7-8	9-12	10-55	12-21	13-43	15-16	17-9	19-23	21-45	0-5	2-26
12	4-44	7-4	9-8	10-51	12-17	13-39	15-12	17-5	19-19	21-41	0-1	2-22
13	4-40	7-0	9-4	10-47	12-13	13-35	15-8	17-1	19-15	21-37	23-57	2-18
14	4-36	6-56	9-0	10-43	12-9	13-31	15-4	16-57	19-11	21-33	23-53	2-14
15	4-32	6-52	8-56	10-39	12-5	13-27	15-0	16-53	19-7	21-29	23-49	2-10
16	4-28	6-48	8-52	10-35	12-1	13-23	14-56	16-49	19-3	21-25	23-45	2-6
17	4-24	6-44	8-48	10-31	11-57	13-19	14-52	16-45	18-59	21-21	23-41	2-2
18	4-20	6-40	8-44	10-27	11-53	13-15	14-48	16-41	18-55	21-17	23-37	1-58
19	4-16	6-36	8-40	10-23	11-49	13-11	14-44	16-37	18-51	21-13	23-33	1-54
20	4-12	6-32	8-36	10-19	11-45	13-7	14-40	16-33	18-47	21-9	23-29	1-50
21	4-8	6-28	8-32	10-15	11-41	13-3	14-36	16-29	18-43	21-5	23-25	1-46
22	4-4	6-24	8-28	10-11	11-37	12-59	14-32	16-25	18-39	21-1	23-21	1-42
23	4-0	6-20	8-24	10-7	11-33	12-55	14-28	16-21	18-35	20-57	23-17	1-38
24	3-56	6-16	8-20	10-3	11-29	12-51	14-24	16-17	18-31	20-53	23-13	1-34
25	3-52	6-12	8-16	9-59	11-25	12-47	14-20	16-13	18-27	20-49	23-9	1-30
26	3-48	6-8	8-12	9-55	11-21	12-43	14-16	16-9	18-23	20-45	23-5	1-26
27	3-44	6-4	8-8	9-51	11-17	12-39	14-12	16-5	18-19	20-41	23-1	1-22
28	3-40	6-0	8-4	9-47	11-13	12-35	14-8	16-1	18-15	20-37	22-57	1-18
29	3-36	5-56	8-0	9-43	11-9	12-31	14-4	15-57	18-11	20-33	22-53	1-14
30	3-32	5-52	7-56	9-39	11-5	12-27	14-0	15-53	18-7	20-29	22-49	1-10
31	3-28	5-48	7-52	9-35	11-1	12-23	13-56	15-49	18-3	20-25	22-45	1-6